A Brief History of the Institute of Chartered Accountants of Jamaica, 1965–2016

A Brief History *— of —* THE INSTITUTE OF CHARTERED ACCOUNTANTS OF JAMAICA, 1965–2016

Patrick E. Bryan

Canoe Press

Jamaica • Barbados • Trinidad and Tobago

ICAJ

Canoe Press
7A Gibraltar Hall Road, Mona
Kingston 7, Jamaica
www.uwipress.com

A catalogue record of this book is available
from the National Library of Jamaica.

ISBN: 978-976-653-028-0 (print)
978-976-653-030-3 (ePub)

Printed in the United States of America

To the Young Turks – Philmore Ogle, Carroll Thorburn, Vernon Chang-Alloy, William Thwaites, James Lord, Alfred Rattray, Linton Minott, Horace Hardy-Henry, Jack Ashenheim, and Denis Goldson and the other founding fathers.

Contents

Illustrations

Tables

Foreword

I had the honour of becoming president of the Institute of Chartered Accountants of Jamaica (ICAJ) in its fiftieth year in 2015. The inspiration to write this book came from two sources. First, during the Fiftieth Anniversary Celebration Brunch in January 2015, at my table were Philmore Ogle, Denis Goldson, Lisa Cousins and Suzette Scott, and Philmore was giving us some history of the ICAJ building. Then it was mentioned and agreed at the table that it would be good to capture a comprehensive history of the ICAJ especially as it was our fiftieth year. I noted the suggestion as a good one.

Second, sometime later when I became president in July 2015, Elaine Robinson (then secretary) and I went to visit Jasper Burnett (past president and ICAJ Distinguished Member) at his Beverly Hills home. Jasper had invited us to his home to discuss the fact that he had a lot of historical material and knowledge on the ICAJ, and he wanted to share as much of that knowledge as possible because, in his own words, "I don't have a lot of time left." It was during that visit that Jasper suggested that a book on the first fifty years be written. He argued that this work would build on previous works on the history of the ICAJ. I again found the idea to be an excellent one for the same reason mentioned at the fiftieth anniversary brunch – not long after, I brought the idea to the Council, which approved the book project.

There are a number of persons to be thanked for making this book a reality, and we would run out of space to list them all. However, there are some persons to whom I would like to give special recognition. The late Angela Reid-Gordon must be recognized for her sterling contribution in helping to coordinate the early administrative details of getting the project up and running. I would like to thank Professor Patrick Bryan for taking on the challenge of writing the history in such an engaging and practical manner; the late Jasper

Burnett for helping to plant the idea of the book (as mentioned before), for giving interviews and for providing historical material; Philmore Ogle who also provided great historical material and for giving interviews for the book; a number of past presidents who gave interviews and ideas; the ICAJ Council; the ICAJ Secretariat staff led by Rosemarie Heaven; and the Public Relations and Publications Committee.

I would like to mention a number of important facts and items that have occurred since the initiation of this book project in 2015. The following individuals were awarded the ICAJ Distinguished Member Award: Leighton McKnight (2017), C. Patricia Hayle (2018) and Adrian Strachan (2019). The following individuals became ICAJ presidents: Raymond Campbell and Sixto Coy. The Institute also formed a number of strategic partnerships with local and overseas bodies. These partnerships, in general, were meant to provide greater access to training facilities to members and students and to give the ICAJ a greater voice on critical issues. A key partnership with the tax authorities was formalized in a memorandum of understanding signed in November 2017.

Bruce Scott
August 2020

Preface

This brief history is intended to record why and how the Institute of Chartered Accountants of Jamaica (ICAJ, Institute) came into being in 1965, and how it has evolved over the years in response to both national and international constraints and opportunities. At the root of accountancy is the increasingly scientific response to the auditing needs of a growing business civilization, notorious for its unpredictability and uncertain about its ethics. In the process, I have devoted some attention to how the Institute's programme for training Jamaican accountants was balanced by the equally important task of mobilizing its expertise to inform public opinion and to make an input into government policy. In the broader historical perspective, the experience of the ICAJ is a microcosm of the wider process of decolonization.

This history combines a chronological and thematic approach. Some overlap was unavoidable, primarily because some issues emerged and re-emerged in the march of the Institute's history.

The first chapter discusses, briefly, the role of "accountancy" in Jamaica prior to 1965. The second chapter outlines the foundations and structure of the Institute of Chartered Accountants of Jamaica. The third chapter focuses on the consolidation of the Institute between 1975 and 1989, the organization's response to macro-economic and political variables, as well as initiatives taken to extend the vision and functions of the organization. The fourth chapter examines the Institute's vision to indigenize the profession. The fifth chapter examines the involvement of the Institute in the foundation of the Institute of Chartered Accountants of the Caribbean (ICAC), as well as the latter's attempted role in indigenization – a process partly stimulated by a vision of Caribbean integration. The sixth chapter discusses the impact of globalization and Jamaica's internal financial crisis on the Institute, which committed itself to globalization of the profession and internal reform. The seventh chapter discusses the development of the student sector. The eighth chapter comments mostly on contemporary social aspects of the organization and is followed by the conclusion.

Acknowledgements

I thank the ICAJ for inviting me to document its history. It has been a rewarding, exciting and challenging experience, which gave me the opportunity to appreciate the outlook of Jamaicans who set out boldly and with nationalistic fervour in the 1950s to establish the foundations of an indigenous accountancy profession. Thanks are due to many people, but I wish to highlight a few:

- The past presidents of the ICAJ who agreed to be interviewed. I mention Mr Philmore Ogle, in particular, because he was not only one of the early presidents but was also one of the founding fathers of the Institute. He has not lost his memory, his fire or his good humour. Mr Ogle made his considerable collection of documents pertaining to the history of the Institute available, documents that are extremely important for the history of the Institute's early years.
- Mr Jasper Burnett, whom I interviewed twice before his recent death, was one of the longest-serving members of the Institute and gave me complete access to those of his files that had not been previously turned over to the Institute.
- The executive director of the ICAJ, Mrs Rosemarie Heaven, who carried her formidable responsibilities with good cheer.
- Mrs C. Patricia Hayle, Mr Bruce Scott, Mr Donald Reynolds (past presidents of the ICAJ) and executive director of the ICAJ, Mrs Rosemarie Heaven, for their comments on a draft of the manuscript.
- The late Mrs Angela Reid-Gordon, who conscientiously provided the thousands of relevant documents housed at the Institute, made all the appointments for the interviews, and who took a lively interest in the study.

- Miss Maxine Francis for continuing the work of the late Mrs Angela Reid Gordon.
- Miss Maxine McDonough for her thorough editorial work.
- The ancillary staff and receptionists, who were invariably courteous, attentive, friendly and helpful.

Abbreviations

AAT	Association of Accounting Technicians
ACA	Associate Chartered Accountant
ACCA	Association of Chartered Certified Accountants
AIA	Association of International Accountants
AICPA	American Institute of Certified Public Accountants
BICA	Bahamas Institute of Chartered Accountants
CACA	Chartered Association of Certified Accountants
CAST	College of Arts Science and Technology
CAT	Certified Accounting Technician
CGA	Certified General Accountants Association of Canada
CICA	Canadian Institute of Chartered Accountants
CIMA	Chartered Institute of Management Accountants
CIPFA	Chartered Institute of Public Finance and Accountancy
CM	*Council Minutes*
CMA	Certified Management Accountants Canada
CPA	Certified Public Accountant
CPD	Continuing Professional Development
CPE	Continuing Professional Education
CSME	Caribbean Single Market and Economy.
FINSAC	Financial Sector Adjustment Company

GATS	General Agreement on Trade in Services
IAS	Institute of Accounting Staff
IASC	International Accounting Standards Committee
ICAB	Institute of Chartered Accountants of Barbados
ICAC	Institute of Chartered Accountants of the Caribbean
ICAEW	Institute of Chartered Accountants of England and Wales
ICAG	Institute of Chartered Accountants of Guyana
ICAI	Institute of Chartered Accountants of Ireland
ICAJ	Institute of Chartered Accountants of Jamaica
ICAJ-N	*ICAJ Newsletter*
ICAS	Institute of Chartered Accountants of Scotland
ICATT	Institute of Chartered Accountants of Trinidad and Tobago
IES	International Educational Standards
IFAC	International Federation of Accountants
IFRS	International Financial Reporting Standards
IPSAS	International Public Sector Accounting Standards
JAPSA	Jamaica Association of Public Sector Auditors
PAA	Public Accountancy Act
PAB	Public Accountancy Board
PSOJ	Private Sector Organisation of Jamaica
RPA	Registered Public Accountant
TCISPA	Turks and Caicos Islands Society of Professional Accountants
UCWI	University College of the West Indies
UTech	University of Technology
UWI	University of the West Indies
WTO	World Trade Organization

Chapter 1

The Background

This chapter reviews the experience of the accounting profession in Jamaica from the colonial period through to the foundation of the Institute of Chartered Accountants of Jamaica on 18 January 1965.

The Colonial Period

Accountancy in Jamaica, whether under the Spaniards (1494 to 1655) or the British (1655 to 1962) was linked to Jamaica's colonial status. We know very little about accountancy in the Spanish period, except that there was an island treasurer with responsibility for the treasury's box with three keys, and that an auditor, sent from Cuba in 1536, placed the island's treasurer, Pedro Mazuelo, in chains.[1] Subsistence production, a livestock industry, and the export of lard under the Spaniards evidently produced little to be accounted for.

For obvious reasons, the over 300 years of the British colonial period exercised the most important influences on the keeping of accounts. Accountancy (as a practice rather than as a profession) came to Jamaica with the establishment of the sugar and coffee plantations, livestock enterprises, rum manufacture and other lesser enterprises all based, up to 1838, on enslaved labour. Jamaica also became an entrepôt for the export of enslaved Africans to the Spanish American Empire. Prosperous business enterprises, based on free enterprise plantations of sugar and coffee, generated an increasingly greater need for a systematic accounting practice. Absentee planters, resident in Britain, required accounts that would keep them up to date on the financial condition of their Jamaican properties. "From 1740 to 1927 all persons acting for owners who were absentees, minors, lunatics, heirs or otherwise not directly in control of their properties, or deceased, were required to return annual accounts of their produce to the Island Secretary."[2] These records, which long preceded the formal establishment of accountancy institutions, have been critically important for the recording of the economic history of Jamaica.

Accounting became less concerned about import and export duties and ad valorem taxes that typified the Spanish period. Accounts were directly related to the management of plantations, which were elaborate agricultural and manufacturing enterprises that encompassed planting, reaping, transportation of cut cane, and processing of molasses, sugar and rum in factories. Accounts in Jamaica, during the period of enslavement, reflected the nature of plantation production: personnel, stock (the enslaved and animal stock), production (sometimes separate books for the boiling and still houses), and exports of hogsheads of sugar, puncheons of rum and bags of coffee. In the 100 years between 1750 and 1850, the plantation books recorded produce despatched from the estates or exported overseas, goods and services acquired, and the number of free and enslaved persons on properties, the health of the enslaved, slave births and deaths, the number of hogsheads of sugar produced for export or, as the case may be, puncheons of rum produced and exported. They also reveal the importance of the ties with the metropolis where merchant creditors' accounts complemented those from across the Atlantic.[3] Jamaican planters, often Englishmen (and Scotsmen) resident in Jamaica as a proprietary class, were often heavily indebted to metropolitan merchants, who recorded how they disposed of the goods imported into Britain from their Jamaican clients, and the relevant payments on the debts owed.

The local record keeper was not usually the so-called bookkeeper (who rarely kept books) but, more often than not, the planter attorney or the overseer. However, "profit and loss accounts, cost analysis and balance sheets are hard to find in British estate accounts down to 1800, though there are important exceptions".[4] "There were practices in Jamaica that not only varied from English practice, but were also regarded as bordering on roguery."[5]

There are occasional glimpses of accounts that were badly or dubiously kept. A recent study reveals cases of a combination of poor accounting and roguery in Jamaica, partly arising from the fact that attorneys' and overseers' private businesses were sometimes in competition with the estates for which they were responsible.[6] In 1809, "a significant error was discovered in the accounts compiled by attorney Rowland Fearon. The computation of Fearon's commission of 6 per cent should have been on the net profits rather than on the gross." It also came to light in 1820 that the accounts of the wealthy Mr Tharp were incorrect and in need of serious auditing.[7]

Keeping of books in colonial Jamaica was not confined to recording or reporting on agricultural and industrial production. On the margins of the plantation economy there was an increasingly important community of shopkeepers and merchants. The story of the mercantile community's accounting in Jamaica during the nineteenth century proved to be, in part, the story of power relations among people in a society that was segmented by race, colour and economic inequalities. Merchants' books, in accordance with the law, not only recorded stock and sales but also the charges levied on small-scale producers who obtained credit from merchants and shopkeepers while awaiting the harvest. The merchants recorded the credit offered to the small holder on the basis of the projected value of the latter's crops. It was the merchant who computed the value of the crop. Justice Gibbons reported in 1884 on the practice among local merchants of "suing" small holders "for balances of account" and how merchants relied upon the absence of the defendant to obtain judgment. He established that some storekeepers used their privileged position to deceive their less educated clients. Some small holders who had used their lands as collateral lost their land to merchants. Justice Gibbons, who had considerable sympathy for the small holders, demanded that the merchants present their books to show how balances had been computed. Merchants were, generally, extremely reluctant to do so. Justice Gibbons observed:

> This, so reasonable itself and so necessary where the defendant is in almost every case an illiterate and uneducated man, appears to have given great dissatisfaction and at Falmouth I was presented with a memorial signed by almost every merchant and shopkeeper there praying that I should forgo the requirement. . . . It was impossible not to see that in many cases advantage had been taken of the ignorance of the debtor but not in all. There was one, and only one, merchant (Mr Levy of Browns Town) whose books were produced without hesitation and

> whose accounts sustained the fullest scrutiny. When it is found that the storekeeper supplies goods at his own price to the cultivator on the credit of his crops and takes produce at his own valuations, it will be manifest that the account between the parties ought to be examined item by item.[8]

Plantation accounts (accounts and produce) and other business accounts documented plantation or mercantile inputs and outputs. The colonial state had its own books to balance – the auditor's department, the tax offices, the public works department and other departments of the colonial state. In addition, the vestries (municipalities), far more important than they are now, were not merely municipal reflections of central government but, in their own right, collectors of revenue.

The Age of Liberalism, 1870–1930

The practice and the prestige of accountancy grew significantly between *circa* 1870 and 1930 – the so-called Age of Liberalism – which witnessed the surge of accountancy as a profession in Britain and the United States of America. Scotland appears to have taken the lead in 1854 to establish accountancy as a legitimate and honourable profession, in association with the legal profession. The growth of accountancy was intimately linked with the international movement of capital and the tremendous expansion of world trade which had been facilitated by major technological changes in transportation (railroads and refrigerated steamships), in communication (the telegraph and telephone), in manufacture (new processes for the smelting of iron ore), new uses for old products (for example the chocolate industry), and scientific agriculture. The managerial revolution and the centrality of finance over industrial capital gave room for the growth of management by technocrats, including accountants. Just over one hundred years later, rapid changes in communication technology wrought significant changes in management and in accountancy. The "Golden Age of Liberalism", emerging out of, and simultaneously with, a scientific revolution, had encouraged the relatively freer movement of capital (and personnel) than had been the case under the old mercantilist economies that favoured protectionism. At the centre of the expansion of accountancy as a profession was Great Britain, easily the largest exporter of capital and perhaps of accountants at the end of the nineteenth century. Equally important was that in the latter half of the nineteenth century there was a tightening of the sentimental, economic and cultural bonds of empire. British influence, under the long reign of Queen Victoria, was the function of an expanding empire that covered sections of the African and Asian continents, the Indian sub-continent, Australia and, of course, the Caribbean. By 1930, there were at least seventeen accountancy bodies in existence in the United Kingdom that serviced the accounting needs of the British Empire.[9]

To a considerable extent the nomadic movement of accountants in the British Empire confirmed that the latter was a tributary empire, which became the undisputed turf for British accountants overseas. The Institute of Chartered Accountants of England and Wales (ICAEW) came into being in 1880. In an age when British capital dominated the international economy, the ICAEW dominated "the most lucrative sectors of the accountancy market in England" and became the "elite body of practitioners".[10] The ICAEW exported its accountants to wherever British capital found itself in the vast British Empire (including Jamaica).

The Association of Chartered Certified Accountants (ACCA), ICAEW, Institute of Chartered Accountants of Scotland (ICAS) and the Institute of Chartered Accountants of Ireland (ICAI 1888) were among the growing number of accounting firms in the United Kingdom during the Liberal Period. The interests of the profession and the latter's prestige were advanced towards the end of the nineteenth century by the publication of several books and journals on accountancy, indicating a professionalization of the field. The expansion of the Jamaican economy, partly attributable to the growth of the banana industry during the first half of the twentieth century, generated a demand for accountants. But, the doors were not yet open to Jamaican participation in the accounting profession. Like architects and engineers, Jamaican accountants were relatively rare.

The ACCA was destined to play a central role in accountancy in Jamaica. It differed from the ICAEW in one important respect: the ACCA was, first and foremost, an examination body for prospective accountants in the British Empire. It organized examination centres in India, Ghana, Nigeria, Hong Kong and Ceylon (Sri Lanka).[11] The ACCA conducted its first examinations in Jamaica in 1915. It also extended its influence over the empire by "exporting credible examinations".[12]

The ACCA's role as examiner was consistent with the role of other (non-accounting) examining bodies in the British Empire from the end of the nineteenth century. A notable feature of the late nineteenth century was the introduction of British examinations into Jamaica. Jamaican students, for example, first sat the Cambridge Examinations in 1882 in Jamaica, reducing the need for studies in the United Kingdom. In 1887, the Institute of Jamaica founded the Cambridge Local Examinations Committee as an agent of the UK-based Cambridge Local Examinations Syndicate, which set and marked high school examinations such as the Cambridge School Certificate and the Higher School Certificate. Jamaicans could also sit the Associated Board of Music Examinations as of 1908. City and Guilds (1905) examinations were conducted at the Manual Training School in Kingston.[13] The University of London also set examinations that enabled Jamaicans and other Caribbean people to obtain degrees (externally) from the University of London at undergraduate and, by the 1920s, graduate levels. ACCA examinations, therefore, corresponded to the new educational/examination norms.

Meanwhile, accounting firms such as PriceWaterhouseCoopers (1916), and Pannell Fitzpatrick Forster (which later became Ernst and Young) counted among the Big Four contemporary international firms that set up offices in Jamaica. In Jamaica, Ivan S. Heron established his Ivan S. Heron, Accountants and Auditors in 1949. In 1955, with Carroll Thorburn joining the firm, it became Heron, Thorburn and Company. Later, the firm became integrated with Deloitte and Touche.[14]

The Great Depression 1930s

The Age of Liberalism ended with the international economic crisis of the 1930s. Since accountancy reacts to business, and not the other way around, the crisis led to the revision of accountancy procedures. While accountants (particularly in the United States) did not accept the principle of "uniform" accounting procedures, some of the major abuses of the 1920s were removed. Furthermore, as enunciated by T. Cristina Maria in an article entitled "The Impact of the Great Depression on American Accountancy Practice": "Rules and regulations that resulted from the Crash of the Stock Market incorporated the use of accountants to audit the corporate entity and in a sense to hold the corporations accountable for their financial transactions. . . . In a sense accountants had become moral guardians for the interest of the public and did a great deal to restore the common citizens' confidence in the business world."[15]

The crisis of the 1930s discredited Golden Age Liberalism and elevated the accountant's role not only as financial advisor, but as "provider of information services".[16] The dream of a revived liberalism remained alive, however, and re-emerged, in modified form, in the 1980s, as neo-liberalism.

Accountancy Institutions in the United Kingdom and in Jamaica before 1965

The anarchic transatlantic and British context influenced the process by which the Institute of Chartered Accountants in Jamaica was established. The accountancy profession in the United Kingdom was disunited. This was due, partly, to competition among the several accounting groups and partly to the hierarchical development of the accounting bodies that placed the ICAEW, the ICAS and to a lesser extent the ICAI in the top tier of the profession, while organizations such as the ACCA, which was wealthy and not without influence, were regarded as outsiders. The term "juniors"[17] was applied to other institutions such as the Association of International Accountants (AIA).

Significant collaboration between accounting bodies and the British government during the crisis of World War II stirred hopes that post-war reconstruction would encourage greater coordination among accounting bodies. The hope that this collaboration would extend to post-war reconstruction was embodied in a serious effort to coordinate the profession during the 1940s. The attempt, which was supported by the ACCA, failed. Disunity continued to mark the accountancy profession in the United Kingdom and, we may add, the profession in Jamaica.[18] A further attempt to coordinate the British profession between 1968 and 1970 also failed as did an effort in 1994.[19] But, "efforts to rationalize the profession faced considerable difficulties, many of which had their foundation in the legacy of separate institutional development which characterizes the history of the accountancy profession. . . . The attempt to coordinate the profession during the 1940s and 1950s reveals that traditional animosities and institutional allegiances were deeply embedded in the psyche of the professional bodies."[20] The ACCA itself lamented that of the great professions (including law and medicine) only the accountancy profession had failed to coordinate its interests.[21]

The result of this historical development was that separate accounting bodies were represented among the accounting fraternity in Jamaica (the ICAEW, ICAS, ICAI and AIA). The accounting bodies in Jamaica did not, and could not, have a unified voice. Accounting firms from the United States also entered Jamaica, following the rapid growth of US commercial influence in the British colony.

With a boom in the accountancy profession in the post-World War II world there was mounting pressure to establish common standards in financial reporting. The boom was no doubt attributable to the post–World War II prosperity induced by an expanding US economy. The "largest accounting firms became increasingly international with longstanding British firms merging with leading North American firms and US firms such as Arthur Andersen opening offices in London and other British cities. . . . The Accountants International Study Group (AISG) was established in 1966 to bring together representatives from the USA, Canada, and the UK in order to identify best accounting practice."[22]

Under the colonial regime, Jamaicans were generally excluded from accountancy and other professions, which were, largely, the domain of expatriates. Resentment of the expatriate bureaucracy was evident from the late nineteenth century, manifested in a tangible antagonism between white (creole) Jamaicans and British "expatriates" who dominated the colonial bureaucracy and a number of professions. The tension is suggested in the works of the novelist Alice Spinner and in the autobiography of W. Adolphe Roberts, who referred to the governor disrespectfully, but with deep feeling, as a "shallow-pated martinet". The "average English official in Jamaica was not admirable", wrote Roberts, who unapologetically referred to Jamaica's crown colony government as "our imported government". Jamaica "had slipped into the third class, being no longer profitable *per se* to England and used chiefly as a place in which jobs could be found for *third-raters*",[23] he wrote. The mixed population also had reason to be discontented. There were wealthy brown Jamaicans, some of whom entered the legal and medical professions, were significant landowners and even held high positions in the public service. However, the greater the progress of the browns the more intense became the social discrimination against them.

There were Jamaicans, however, who were determined to break into the exclusive domain of the accounting profession. In the post-World War II period, a number of West Indians received education and training grants from the British Further Education and Training Programme as a thank you for their war service. Gladstone Mills noted, "Among those were John Clarke, W.S. Richardson, Fred Barrows, Alvin Chapman, Lloyd Johnson, and N.W. Mills, all in accounting."[24] There were also Jamaican secondary school graduates who had gained some experience working at the Income Tax or Auditor General's departments. Others did correspondence courses, joined accounting firms or attended night schools. Other aspiring Jamaican accountants (as well as engineers) also found occupation in the sugar industry, which continued to be a major industry in Jamaica.

Philmore Ogle completed his ACCA in Jamaica through a correspondence course. Uriel Salmon began with a correspondence course, night school (and a teaching job to pay for the correspondence course) and eventually received a government scholarship to enable him to study for his accountancy qualification in the United Kingdom.[25] It is clear, from the experiences of Uriel Salmon and Jasper Burnett, that ambitious black Jamaicans considered being articled to an accounting firm insufficient to ensure rising to the top of the profession as partners. There was little hope of becoming more than a clerk in a large establishment.[26] It has been asserted that some of the expatriate firms were guilty of racial discrimination.

Burnett's stance on racism was not only influenced by local realities but by international racist politics such as existed under apartheid in South Africa. In a letter to W.H. Kruger, executive director, National Council of Chartered Accountants of South Africa, Johannesburg, Burnett declined the invitation to be the guest of the National Council at the National Congress of Accountants in South Africa. Burnett, president of the Institute at the time, declared: "the people of my country are totally opposed to apartheid. . . . If, however, your government and people should abandon this monstrous denial of basic human rights . . . we shall be happy to visit."[27] The most viable course for those anxious to become accountants was a costly sojourn in Britain. Carroll Thorburn, who started as a functionary in the Ivan Heron accounting firm, earned his ACCA overseas.[28]

Jasper Burnett, a pupil teacher turned member of the Jamaican Constabulary Force, was fortunate enough to receive private financial support for accountancy studies in Britain in 1955. For black Jamaicans there was little prospect of professional occupations beyond primary school teaching, the religious ministry, or the Jamaica Constabulary Force, whose upper ranks were, in any case, reserved both by law and convention for British expatriates. In the absence of a university (until the University College of the West Indies [UCWI] was opened in 1948) graduate degrees were obtained either by studies in Britain, or by correspondence courses from UK-based institutions. Very few people (under five per annum) graduated in accountancy from local accounting institutions. It is, therefore, with only limited exaggeration that Everton McDonald, upon receiving the distinguished award of the Institute of Chartered Accountants of Jamaica in December 2013, could declare that "In the late sixties and early seventies, it was almost a national event when two or three persons qualified as Accountants in a year. On average we now have over 60 . . . in a year for the last 20 years. [It] made it possible for thousands like myself to study at home as against going to the UK and achieve an internationally recognised accountancy qualification."[29]

Lack of opportunity in the accounting profession in Jamaica was therefore seen both through the lens of nationalism and the lens of race. Both creole and black nationalists shared, for slightly different reasons, antagonism to the overt policy of exclusion. The common enemy was the expatriate bureaucracy.

Concerns for a Jamaican-controlled profession reflected the growing national consciousness – already exemplified in such institutions as Jamaica Welfare – a growing awareness of Jamaican arts and culture and, since universal adult suffrage in the 1940s, political populism. Tensions in Jamaican society did not arise only between colour tiers but between white creole Jamaicans and expatriate white Jamaicans, closely paralleling the animosities between creole and metropolitan whites in colonial Spanish America.

There is a small body of literature that indicates that aspirations to join the civil service, of which expatriate accountants constituted a substantial proportion, were central to the dissatisfaction with the colonial regime, whose policy of exclusion made it difficult for Jamaicans to hold important office in the civil service. In his autobiography, Gladstone Mills writes about the obstacles to occupational advancement by Jamaicans:

> During the 1930s, for entry to the civil service an applicant was required to have passed the Cambridge School Certificate examination with a G (Good) or C (Credit) in English and Maths and to hold a certificate of the London University Matriculation examination. The applicant was also required to submit a recommendation from a member of the Privy Council, the Custos of his parish of residence, a member of the legislative council, or the head of a civil service department, certifying him as a fit and proper person for admission to the service. In addition to these there was a competitive examination, arranged once each year, comprising précis writing, composition, dictation, handwriting, arithmetic and bookkeeping, general knowledge of Jamaica and correction of errors in expression.[30]

To obtain expertise in bookkeeping, Mills enrolled at Durham College of Commerce. The civil service, the upper reaches of the Jamaica Constabulary Force and employment in high schools were all reserved, for the most part, for expatriates, who viewed their presence in Jamaica as temporary.

Philmore Ogle, a strong advocate for a Jamaican accountancy profession, claimed in November 1968 that only about two new chartered accountants were produced each year in Jamaica compared to a demand for over three hundred accountants. Ogle, himself a high school graduate, had done his ACCA in Jamaica through a correspondence course. The rapid expansion of businesses in Jamaica during the post–World War II period increased the demand for accountants in the island.

To some extent, the Jamaican experience of accountancy was a reflection of the international post–World War II economic order. Jamaica was caught between two empires: the British empire of sugar, molasses and rum and the US empire of bananas, bauxite/alumina, aviation, hotels and tourism. The entry of US corporations "provided opportunities for some states of America to establish centres for the preparation of the American Institute of Certified Public Accountants (AICPA) final examinations in Jamaica. The AICPA final examinations were to be held in centres in America."[31] Finance capital from the United States, which "catapulted Accountancy into being an 'international' profession and intensified the drive for global congruence in accounting practice".[32] The rising demand for accountants in Jamaica following World War II continued to be met by recruiting accountants from North America and Britain. As we will see, however, the British dominance of the accounting profession continued in Jamaica. The advancement of the profession in Jamaica is, in part, the story of the ACCA, in part, the story of voluntary associations in Jamaica and, in part, a nationalistic attempt to establish a Jamaican-based profession. Decolonization did not take place only at the political/constitutional level.

Healthy exports of bananas and sugar to the United Kingdom continued, but since the 1950s, US economic influences had been outstripping British participation in the economy and grew even more rapidly after political independence in 1962. The expansion of business in Jamaica in the 1950s and 1960s was spearheaded by heavy investments in the export sector and associated infrastructural developments. Bauxite and alumina production, which were the province of US- and Canadian-based corporations, underscored the impact of US financial capital on Jamaica. Developments in aviation included the construction of two new international airports. Bauxite/alumina, tourism and hotels were all part of the extension of the US informal empire into Jamaica and the Caribbean. Hemispheric economic sanctions against Cuba, following the 1959 Revolution, facilitated the export of sugar to the United States. The number of registered companies in Jamaica multiplied.[33]

The 1950s and 1960s were "good" economic times, at least for the wealthy. Often, if not always, at the forefront of the collective mind of the advocates of a Jamaican accounting body was the extent to which Jamaicans could reap the fruits of an internationally induced prosperity. Economic growth in Jamaica had not brought about a flowering of the accountancy profession. The field continued to be dominated by expatriates. It all seemed to confirm the cynical but, nevertheless, meaningful comment made by Prime Minister Benjamin Disraeli of Britain in the late nineteenth century: "A colony does not cease to be a colony because it is independent."

Although it is true that the UK-based Association of Chartered Certified Accountants (ACCA) had established an Examination Centre in Jamaica in 1915, and a branch of the ACCA in 1948, the accounting profession in Jamaica in the 1950s and 1960s was dominated by expatriate individuals and firms originating from the United Kingdom and the United States. Pannell Fitzpatrick had set up offices in Jamaica from the 1920s. There were a few local firms in

Jamaica and in Trinidad and Tobago, for example, Ivan Heron in Jamaica and John Hunt in Trinidad and Tobago. Both were later to be absorbed by larger expatriate firms – Hunt's firm in 1972 by Coopers Lybrand and Heron's firm by Deloitte Touche.[34] Even with the energies released by universal adult suffrage in 1944, Jamaica was still very much a British colony, albeit in the process of "decolonization". This reality was not reflected only in the accountancy profession. It applied equally, or almost equally, to other occupations: high school teaching, architecture, the public service and engineering. Another reminder of that reality was the tendency for segments of the civil service to be dominated by expatriates, many of them functionaries of the crown colony government that came to an end, constitutionally, in 1962.

Yet, there were Jamaicans, before independence in 1962, who questioned the accountancy status quo in Jamaica. One of the initiatives taken by Philmore Ogle and Carroll Thorburn (who were among the most militant) was to persuade the Extra Mural Department of the UCWI to include accountancy in its curriculum offered in the corporate area and Montego Bay starting in 1960. This was the modest beginning of a training programme for potential accountants in Jamaica and the beginning of a continuous, but sometimes thorny, relationship between the UCWI/UWI and the Institute of Chartered Accountants of Jamaica. In 1962, the ACCA "agreed to allow accountants in Jamaica to mark examination papers in anticipation of, and in preparation for, a Jamaican body eventually taking over completely" from the ACCA.[35] It seemed, then, that those who favoured the Jamaicanization of the profession would enjoy the support of the ACCA.

In the following chapter, I outline how Jamaicans succeeded in establishing the ICAJ.

Chapter 2

The Foundations of the Institute of Chartered Accountants of Jamaica

The establishment of a Jamaican accountancy profession was driven by nationalism and by the pragmatic recognition that there were significant employment opportunities for qualified Jamaican accountants. At the forefront of the agitation, which began in the mid to late 1950s, were Philmore Ogle, Carroll Thorburn, William Thwaites and seventeen others who signed up.

2.1 William Thwaites, one of the founding fathers of the Institute and president, 1965–68

2.2 Philmore Ogle, president, 1968–70 – one of the "young Turks" with a passionate belief in the establishment of a Jamaican-based accountancy profession

Under the umbrella of nationalism there were four major, and to some extent overlapping, objectives. The first, and probably the most important, objective in the short term was the unification and legal incorporation of the accounting profession in Jamaica. The second was the training of more accountants in Jamaica and, simultaneously, the reduction of expatriate domination of the field. The third was to orient the profession to meet the developmental needs of Jamaica. The fourth was the indigenization of the profession with its own regulations, examinations, certification and ethics.[1]

On the eve of political independence in 1962, the accountancy profession in Jamaica (like the UK profession) was disunited. It is probable that many of the animosities that accompanied the unification of the profession in Jamaica from the late 1950s to the 1960s signified a reflection of pre-existing rivalries among the UK-based accounting bodies that were represented in Jamaica.

There were about five accounting bodies in Jamaica in 1960: the Jamaica District of the Association of Certified Accountants, affiliated with the ACCA; the Society of Chartered Accountants of Jamaica, which included members of the ICAEW; the Institute of Accountants of Scotland; the Institute of Chartered Accountants of Canada and the Association of Accountants of Jamaica. Institutional agitation for the establishment of a unified body of accountants in Jamaica probably began with the formation by Jamaicans of the Association of Accountants of Jamaica Inc. (1958–1965). The latter association was the predecessor of the ICAJ.

Philmore Ogle, who was the last president of the AAJ Inc., summarized his view of the association's role in the following way:

> The Association of Accountants of Jamaica Inc. was a hotchpotch of any and sundry persons who professed to be accountants – except for those who preferred not to become members. It had no status, standard or authority. An early purpose of the Young Turks was to put it out of misery, and they did so in two moves. The first was to install Carroll Thorburn as president. The second was to elect Philmore Ogle as its last president, and all he was called on to do was to preside over the meeting which resolved to appoint the late Mr. J.A. Capleton as liquidator.[2]

The AAJ handed over its assets ($939.24) to the ICAJ in 1973.[3]

Discussions leading to the unification of the profession proved acrimonious, especially between the "chartered" and "certified" accountants. The main

2.3 Carroll Thorburn presents to UWI's vice-chancellor Phillip Sherlock the Deeds of the Covenant to finance for five years the cost of a lecturer for accounting at UWI, October 1, 1964. Also in picture at centre is Hon. Hector Wynter, UWI Registrar. At extreme right is Jim F.L. Lord, who served as president of the ICAJ, 1970–71.

argument in favour of unification of the accounting profession was that it was a precondition for uniformity of standards and a collective authoritative voice for the profession. With three major bodies representing the profession, there was no guarantee of a collective authoritative voice for the profession. Two of the associations were structurally linked with their overseas counterparts. The agitators had in mind questions of legislation, including taxation. Of particular concern was the Companies Act (1965), which had been imposed without consultation with the accounting bodies.[4] In short, the ability of accountants to act as a lobbying group would have greater success as a unit.

Opportunities for training in Jamaica, it was generally understood, were very limited. The rhetoric of the "Young Turks", as Philmore Ogle and his team were dubbed, was couched in nationalist terms and philosophically shared the opposition of Jamaicans to their exclusion from power and opportunity from the late nineteenth century. The "nationalist" orientation of Jamaican accountants mirrored a deep-seated antagonism to expatriate domination of the civil service and other "responsible offices".

In 1962, following extensive discussions among the accounting firms, the agitators took the initiative to frame a bill that proposed the legal framework for an Institute of Chartered Accountants of Jamaica. The draft of the proposed bill, based on legal precedents from jurisdictions outside Jamaica, was composed by Philmore Ogle. The agitators found a champion in minister of trade and industry Robert Lightbourne, who carried it forward. In 1963, the Ministry of Trade and Industry advocated the reduction of foreign domination of the profession and the promotion of nationalism, and agreed to enact a Public Accountancy Act to defend the interests of Jamaican accountants.[5] Robert Lightbourne's declaration that the "accountancy profession was perhaps the profession which expanded in the closest ratio with the economic development of Jamaica" and that there was a "tremendous expansion of the profession in recent years" signalled moral and legislative support for Jamaican accountants from the Jamaican government.[6] Lightbourne's memorable declaration that "A developing Jamaica and a growing accountancy profession are like rice and peas, the one cannot get along in any way without the other" indicated his agreement with the agitators that the profession needed to have a local flavour.[7] The proposed law's original intention, which was to boost the number of Jamaican accountants, was reinforced by a Work Permit Law in 1964.

The Jamaican government also tried to ease the shortage of Jamaican accountants by offering scholarships for training in Britain, and by encouraging the private sector to do likewise. These scholarships were useful but not sufficiently abundant to fill the need for at least three hundred accountants in Jamaica. The gap had to be closed by importation.

The successful passage of the bill (with Lightbourne's support) enabled the now unified profession to be incorporated under the Companies' Act on 18 January 1965 as the Institute of Chartered Accountants of Jamaica. The term "Chartered" (rather than "Certified") was selected because it was the term "better known in the Commonwealth".[8] The heraldic insignia of the ICAJ was designed as a shield with the motto, *Vere et Digne*. The shield, depicting the Jamaican crocodile and three pineapples, reflected the Institute's Jamaican roots. The three pineapples represent the three most important accounting bodies, including the AAJ Inc. The designers of the logo were Jamaicans because the charge of 250 guineas (£262) by the College of Heraldry in London was out of the financial reach of the ICAJ.

2.4 Minister Robert Lightbourne (centre) receiving Articles of Association from a delegation of ICAJ Founding Members. Left to right: Alvin McClure, Trevor Brown, Alfred Rattray, Horace Hardy-Henry, William Thwaites and Philmore Ogle, 23 February 1965. (This was the first official duty performed by the ICAJ.)

2.5 Logo of the ICAJ

The ICAJ started with twenty members. The choice of chartered accountant William Thwaites (1965–68) and the certified accountant Philmore Ogle (1968–70) as the first two presidents symbolized the reconciliation between the "chartered" and the "certified".

ICAJ and PAB

The incorporation of the ICAJ on 18 January 1965 was followed by another important legal step – the formation of a public body with overall responsibility for the regulation of the accountancy profession in Jamaica. This, apparently, was done at the insistence of Philmore Ogle who believed that incorporation under the Companies Act was not sufficient.[9] The result was the passage of the Public Accountancy Act (PAA) that incorporated the Public Accountancy Board (PAB) in 1968. The PAB, which was launched in 1970, was the licensing and regulatory arm of government. The Institute's mandate, under the PAA, included the establishment and monitoring of accounting and auditing standards.

Through the PAA, the Institute was endowed with juridical personality, property rights, and the right to initiate and revise its by-laws (so long as they did not conflict with the PAA). The act outlined the basic responsibilities of the Institute, which were to "promote and increase the knowledge, skill and proficiency of its members and students, and to regulate, discipline and monitor the professional conduct of members and students".[10] The PAA reserved for the Institute the exclusive right to the use of the titles "Chartered Accountant", "Certified Accountant", "Certified Public Accountant" or "Incorporated Accountant".[11] The Institute, through these legal dispensations, enjoyed a powerful position with respect to the regulation and development of the accountancy profession in Jamaica. That power was increased by the statutory arrangement that up to six members of the ICAJ could sit on the Public Accountancy Board, which had ten members. And so, although the Institute operated under the PAB (which was responsible to the minister of finance), the strong presence of the ICAJ on the Public Accountancy Board gave the ICAJ the operational power to regulate, discipline and educate its members and students.

The first chairman of the PAB was Dr Alfred Rattray who was succeeded by Mr Aston Preston, when the former took up a position as Jamaican ambassador in Washington.

The ICAJ and ACCA

The objective of training students in accountancy led to dialogue between the local lobby group on the one hand and the ACCA and Institute of Chartered Accountants of England and Wales (ICAEW) on the other. Of the major accounting bodies, the ICAEW was easily the most powerful and influential both in the United Kingdom and within the British Commonwealth. The ACCA was the "second largest of the four bodies of professional accountants recognized by law in the UK for purposes of statutory audit".[12] Although not as large as the powerful ICAEW, the ACCA had 15,500 members and almost 56,000 students, internationally, in the 1970s.[13] By the end of 2013, the ACCA had 154,000 members and 432,000 students in 170 countries.

The top-tier qualification, the ACCA professional certification, has always been guided by a Joint ICAJ/ACCA examination. The idea of a joint examination emerged during the first year of the Institute's establishment in 1965. In August 1965, the ICAJ and the ACCA agreed to a joint examination in which the name of the Institute would be over-printed on the ACCA's examination papers. The first joint examination took place in June 1966.[14] During the regime of Kenneth Lewis (1983–85), these arrangements were formalized and a bilateral agreement relating to the conduct and discipline of students added.[15]

The joint examination scheme was the first of its kind among accountancy bodies "anywhere in the world".[16] Syllabuses, examinations and exemptions were largely the responsibility of the ACCA. The alliance has proved durable. The association between the ACCA and the ICAJ also extended to the AAT and the CAT, which was introduced in 1997.

The ACCA was selected for several reasons. First, the ACCA, which had established an examination centre in 1915 and a Jamaican branch in 1948, was well known in Jamaica. Its standards were well known and respected. The majority of Caribbean-born accountants were ACCA graduates. Second, the ACCA was considered to be "more inclusive" and international than the ICAEW, which had systematically excluded colonials. As a member of the "Young Turks", Ogle had perhaps not been as diplomatic in the past as he was in the 2017 interview. In 1964, the Young Turks had described the attitude of English Institutions (excluding the ACCA) as a "disgusting reminder of Imperialism".[17]

The ACCA and its predecessor the LAA were "competency bodies whose role was that of certifying expertise. Unlike the chartered bodies, exclusion on the basis of social and cultural capital was not part of the ACCA's operational code". It was an "examinations merchant, which achieved empire domination through the export of credible examinations".[18] In contrast, the ICAEW, which encouraged the export of its members (who undertook tours of duty overseas), augmented its prestige at home. The *modus operandi* of the Institute of Chartered Accountants of England and Wales (ICAEW), in spite of its domination in the British Empire, "did not allow the ICAEW to set examinations outside of its territory".[19] The same exclusiveness applied to the Institute of Chartered Accountants of Ireland and the Institute of Chartered Accountants of Scotland. Some consideration must have been given to US-based credentials, since Ogle concluded that the ACCA was "less prescriptive" than prevailing systems in the United States. The attitude of the English Institutes was not "in keeping with national dignity". The soft-spoken representative of the fledging ICAJ was therefore removed and replaced by an "unyielding nationalist" on 14 November 1964.[20] Indeed, the ACCA proved very helpful and cooperative in the establishment of the ICAJ and seemed sympathetic to the objectives of the Jamaican institution to conduct its own examinations after a period of two or three years.

Curiously enough, in the negotiations towards the establishment of the Caribbean Examinations Council (CXC) (between 1964 and 1979), Jamaica had shown a preference for something of a partnership with Cambridge and London to the extent of having one or the other examining body sit on the projected Council of the CXC. Jamaican negotiators had envisaged a partnership in which "the final product, a GCE Certificate, awarded exclusively by the independent Caribbean Examinations Council, would be accepted by the universities and other bodies in the United Kingdom as equivalent to GCE Certificates awarded by the British Examination Boards".[21] Jamaica was overruled when it was decided that the CXC would become an examining body in its own right, competitive with Cambridge and London. The ACCA/ICAJ Association had a clear precedent in Jamaican thought. The ICAJ became the face of the ACCA in Jamaica. In a memorandum of June 1965 to accounting students, President William Thwaites explained the relationship between the ICAJ and the ACCA:

> Papers [and syllabuses] will be identical with ACCA regular examinations, and so passing these examinations will qualify local students to be graduates of both the Jamaica Institute and the ACCA. Those who pass the Canadian Chartered Accountancy Examinations will also be eligible for membership of the Jamaica Institute. The arrangements with the ACCA are temporary . . . as the Jamaican Institute will develop its own examination questions in course of time.

The Institute, it is claimed, even based its own code of practices on those of the ACCA, which gave the Institute permission to do so.[22] However, the most important aspect of the ICAJ/ACCA agreement was the joint ICAJ/ACCA professional examination in Jamaica. This agreement has continued, though not entirely unchallenged, to the present day. The ICAJ, it can be argued, is offshoot, partner and client of the ACCA.

2.6 Visit to Jamaica of president and secretary of ACCA in 1955

The link between the Jamaican institution and ACCA grew stronger as Jamaican accountants distinguished themselves by becoming formal members of the international ACCA Assembly, which was founded in 1997. The Assembly encouraged international and regional participation in defining general professional standards. As such, the representative regions were offered a voice in the strategic planning process as it affected their regions.[23] Aulous Madden was the first Caribbean Chartered Accountant to be elected to the ACCA International Assembly (1998–99). Other Jamaicans were to follow: C. Patricia Hayle, Prunella Vassell, Raphael Gordon, Leighton McKnight, Eric Crawford and Vintoria Bernard. The international profile of Jamaican accountants has now gone beyond the ACCA. Dennis Brown, honorary treasurer and one of the principal officers of ICAJ, was appointed to the UNCTAD Group on Capacity Building.

2.7 Opening of the ACCA Caribbean Office, July 1999

The ACCA became dominant not only in Jamaica but in other parts of the British colonial and post-colonial societies. The ACCA is strong in Jamaica, Trinidad and Tobago, and Guyana. However, the certified general accountant (CGA) of Canada is prominent in Barbados and the American Institute of Certified Public Accountants (AICPA) in the Bahamas. The idea of a regional body of Caribbean accountants was supported by the ACCA, though an effort by ACCA representatives in 1976 to encourage an Eastern Caribbean association did not bear fruit immediately. The apex body became reality in 1989. In 1978, the ICAJ noted "its appreciation for its [the ACCA's] substantial and positive contribution to the continuing education programme of the Institute".[24] In 1978–79, Jeremy Williams, secretary for overseas relations of the Association of Certified Chartered Accountants (ACCA), became part of a long tradition of visits to the ICAJ, which culminated much later in joint ACCA/ICAJ graduation exercises.[25]

Financing

The strong moral and legal support extended by the government to the Institute did not extend to government subventions. The PAB was silent on the question of financing the growth of the accountancy profession in Jamaica.[26] In the absence of government subventions, ICAJ operated as a voluntary association of chartered accountants, dependent for its regular operations on the subscriptions of its members, the fees of students, payments from the ACCA for services, various fund-raising activities (seminars, graduations, luncheons, ICAC conferences, the *Charter* magazine) and the financial and institutional support of accountancy firms. The latter also offered assistance in kind, "The financial and professional responsibility for accountancy training has continued to devolve on the larger firms, some of whom try to extend their facilities to accommodate students who are not employed by them. It is also to be noted that those firms who cannot themselves fund a training programme generously afford students time off to attend lectures to prepare for the professional examinations."[27] Although the Institute's income, derived from transactions with members and students, is exempt from income tax under the mutuality principle, it is "subject to income tax on investment income and on surplus arising from services to the extent that they relate to transactions with non-members".[28] Voluntarism was a key factor in the emergence of the Institute, but cannot be quantified.

We now turn to the structure of the Institute, which was led by a council of twelve, supported by a number of committees that reflected the specific activities of the Institute.

The Council

The Council of the Institute consisted of a president and vice-president and ten other annually elected members, including at least one member from the public sector. Except for the president and vice-president, the annually elected members of the Council retired by rotation in accordance with By-Law 12 (1) (a). The Council included representation from members who were in public practice, as well as members who were not in public practice. No less than one third of the Council consisted of non-practising members. (Accountants not in practice tend to be employed in larger organizations, but do not have a practising certificate.) In the interest of continuity, there were two conventions: first, each president was entitled to serve for a maximum of two years; second, vice-presidents normally, though not always, succeeded to the presidency.

Unusual circumstances sometimes dictated exceptions to the convention. The first president, William Thwaites (1965–68), engaged in detailed negotiations for the incorporation of the Institute and served for three years to facilitate the consolidation of the new organization. Jasper Burnett served for two and a half years (1977–80) to complete the term of his predecessor who had resigned suddenly. Kenneth La Cruise, Edgar Jones, Jim Lord and Dereck Sale opted for one year only.

In 1978, there were sixteen meetings of the Council for the year. Subsequent to that, there were generally about eleven meetings, barring emergencies. Each member of the Council, having been assigned to chair a specific committee, reported to the Council. The Council, in turn, reported to the annual general meeting, usually held, at least in the first few years, in June each year. The policy of carefully recording attendance in annual reports was a clear indication that the Institute expected regular attendance from the Council's membership.

Participation on the Council was strictly voluntary. "The members of the Council are volunteers. No member of the Council has received payment in respect of services to the Institute, other than by way of reimbursement of incidental expenses incurred in providing such services."[29] The day-to-day operations of the Institute were overseen by an executive of four principal officers: the president, the vice-president, secretary and treasurer.

Committees

The ICAJ early adopted a committee system that reflected the vision for the growth and development, the integrity, and ethical probity of the accountancy profession in Jamaica. These committees, which did much of the groundwork for the Council, were essential for determining strategies for the growth of the profession. There has been considerable continuity in the history of these sub-committees, numbering sixteen in 2016. There was, at the same time, in the early years some experimentation. There are two committees, for example, whose titles are of as much interest as data on them is absent. These are the "Social Aspects of Financial Reporting" (1977) and "Accounting for Small Businesses" (1977). The motivation for establishing them goes unmentioned. It is reasonable to speculate, however, that there were members of the ICAJ who were coming to view their function more broadly to include community welfare. Those two committees, however, appear never to have got off the ground. Committees have been added and sometimes subtracted and sometimes merged. Alterations in the committee structure reflect changes in the organization as well as new demands on the organization through time. For example, in 1977 the Council agreed to establish an audit standards committee in order to relieve the Professional Practice Committee. In order to promote its work in Jamaica, the Institute created a current affairs committee and a publicity committee.

The Institute's credibility was enhanced by the investigative and disciplinary committees that processed cases of violation of by-laws leading to fines, warnings or even expulsions. It was, however, all the committees combined, rather than the investigative and disciplinary committees (as important as these committees were) that helped to ensure the credibility of the Institute.

The audit practice and accounting standards committees were specifically concerned with keeping members up to date in those areas. The by-laws and handbook committees were essential, in a period of consolidation, for the updating of the by-laws and handbook. The frequency with which by-laws were changed, modified or extended, and the need to keep the handbook of the Institute up to date, dictated the formation of specific committees for that purpose. The first handbook, published in 1975 during Alastair Macbeath's regime, codified "all material issued by the Institute since its inception. The contents included the by-laws, a reprint of the Public Accountancy Act, a directory of members, statements of standard accounting practice and recommendations on accounting principles which are issued by the Institute from time to time."[30] The handbook was intended to be the source book of the Institute's authority.

The Finance Committee reported annually on the finances of the Institute that operated on a shoestring budget in the early years. *Charter* magazine, founded and first edited by Jasper Burnett in 1979, was intended to raise funds for the organization and to be a platform for discussions on a wide variety of topics related to the profession.

A newsletter (the first issue of which was published in November 1967) kept members up to date on events and professional matters. The Examinations and Student Registration Committee and the Student Society attended to student affairs.

It was made clear that the Institute's functions went beyond examinations and student affairs. In the 1970s, the ICAJ's Future of the Profession Committee was committed to reducing the "facelessness" of the accounting profession in Jamaica.[31] Its function was to keep members abreast of modern developments and standards, to provide a forum for discussion on matters of moment to the profession and to the business community, and to organise research activity. The Committee for Continuing Education, which was early off the mark, ensured that members were kept up to date on the "the rapidly expanding technological developments in the field of accountancy. That committee, in 1975, developed a project to create a proper library of accountancy literature."[32]

The concept of "mandatory professional development" that became so central to policy making at the end of the twentieth century had already been envisaged by the international accounting fraternity and by the ICAJ in 1977. Phillip Aspinall argued:

> The days when a professional, once qualified, was qualified for life, are all but gone. The explosion of knowledge over the past two decades has rendered many professionals obsolete. The idea that one must continue to update oneself annually in order to continue the right to practice may seem extreme to some, but there is little doubt that this is a phenomenon which is here to stay. . . . Professional inspection/peer revision was a key element in the regulatory programme of professional corporations.[33]

The larger role of the Institute came to include the establishment of taxation, public sector, current affairs committees and a public relations committee. Recruitment to these various committees was a stepping stone to membership of the twelve-person Council.

Membership

Membership of the Institute assumed a professional qualification (such as the ACCA), a defined number of years of experience working in a reputable accounting firm and admission to ICAJ membership by a formal application to the Council of the Institute. The establishment in 1975 of the UWI MSc in Accounting (which we discuss later) opened another route to membership.

Since, however, the ICAJ was founded at the time of Jamaican independence, there were important questions with respect to citizenship. The ICAJ, for all the nationalistic reasons we have mentioned above, favoured Jamaican citizens or persons who were normally resident in Jamaica as a precondition for associate membership. Non-Jamaicans could, however, receive affiliate membership. Resident status and membership of the Institute are required for the public practice of accounting. After various modifications, the ICAJ issued a bulletin to publicize the general qualifications for admission to the ICAJ as full members and to explain the functions and powers of the Institute:

> A Chartered Accountant is a member of the Institute of Chartered Accountants of Jamaica. A Chartered Accountant is not someone who has completed a professional accounting examination. Under the Public Accountancy Act of 1968, the ICAJ is the body responsible for regulating the designations "Chartered Accountant" in Jamaica. The designations indicate that Chartered Accountants are, by training and experience, qualified to provide services in the areas of accounting, auditing, taxation, finance and various aspects of business management. [Members] can be sole practitioners, or in partnership. The Institute offers professional services to a wide variety of clients. Alternatively, they may occupy senior positions in industry, commerce or the public sector. For those,

> whose interests and skills are suited to teaching and research, there are many opportunities available for providing Accountancy training.[34]

Membership of the Institute was divided into the following representative categories.

Table 2.1. Membership of the ICAJ

	1988	1994	1995
Fellow in public practice	$1,100	$6,000	$8,000
Fellow not in public practice	$600	$4,000	$5,500
Associate in public practice	$1,100	$6,000	$8,000
Associate not in public practice (resident firm)	$600	$4,000	$5,500
Member overseas	$500	$4,000	$5,500
Affiliate in public practice (non-resident firm)	$1,100	$12,000	$20,000
Affiliate not in public practice	$500	$6,000	$5,500

(The fees listed are for April 1988, 1994 and 1995. The steady increase in fees, over the years, reflects both Jamaica's inflationary spiral between 1989 and 1994 and the multiplication of activity on the part of the Institute.)

The Institute outlined the qualifications for entry into the ICAJ in the form of a leaflet: "How does one become a Chartered Accountant?":

> Pass any of the qualifying examinations of the Institute: Association of Chartered Certified Accountants (ACCA) Professional Examination; Certified Management Accountant (CMA); Certified General Accountants (CGA); an MSc in Accounting (UWI), or final exam of the American Institute of Certified Public Accountants (AICPA).
>
> Practical experience of no fewer than three years, by working in a professional firm or being engaged in accounting work in sufficiently responsible positions.
>
> Be at least twenty-one years old.
>
> Be recommended by two members of the Institute.
>
> Be admitted to membership by the Council of the Institute.

The accounting profession had not only been an expatriate but also a male domain. However, as in other areas of Jamaican professional life, female involvement grew. There was no law prohibiting female membership of the Institute and, in any case, Law 20 of 1944, "The Sex Disqualification (Removal) Law expressly forbade disqualification on the basis of sex or marriage from the exercise of any public function."[35] However, the fact that there were twenty males and no females affixing their signatures to the articles of association on 18 January 1965 confirmed the tradition or culture of male exclusivity in the accounting profession, at that time.

2.8 Charliana Alexander, FCA, FCCA, the first female chartered accountant registered with the Institute

Charliana Alexander, who registered with the Institute in December 1970, was the first female chartered accountant to be admitted to membership of the ICAJ.[36] To the question of why she chose to enter a male-dominated profession, her simple and modest answer was that she was "good at it".

The first woman to sit on the Institute's Council was Laura Johnson who, having served from June 1977 to February 1978, resigned because of ill health. After some fifty years, female representation in the ICAJ is marginally greater than male membership. Female participation is not confined to the general membership. It extends to leadership of the Institute's committees, membership of Council (in limited numbers until recently) and the presidency of the Institute itself.

Over the fifty years of the Institute's existence three women have served as president, C. Patricia Hayle, Prunella Vassell and Vintoria Bernard – compared with twenty-seven men. Other women have served the profession with distinction: Ethlyn Norton Coke, Gloria Hamilton, Pamela Monroe Ellis, the current auditor general of Jamaica, Caryl Fenton, Allison Peart and Elaine Robinson, honorary secretary to the ICAJ Council. In 2010–11, five of the twelve council members were women. The present executive director of the Institute is Mrs Rosemarie Heaven. The increase of female membership in the accounting profession is a logical development arising from the growth of female education starting from the late nineteenth century that saw women gaining more rapidly in literacy and in high school attendance than their male counterparts. In contemporary times they attend the best high school institutions. Women looked with more interest at the accounting profession from the 1970s. Approximately 80 per cent of women pass their examinations, a fact that is likely to expand the pool of women. In spite of the growing role of women, and a far more visible presence than fifty years ago, female members of the profession believe that they have to struggle against a male bias within the profession. Men do not necessarily agree about the male bias but concede that the gender balance of the accounting profession, as a whole, is being tilted in favour of women.

Membership in the accountancy profession has, occasionally, followed generational lines – such as William Thwaites, Dereck Sale and the Goldson family. Alastair MacBeath, originally from Scotland, noted in an interview that accounting was the preferred profession within his family. However, in more recent times, membership in the profession has been determined mainly by opportunities provided by the expanding Jamaican educational system, especially at the high school, the CAST/UTech and UWI levels.

2.9 Pamela Monroe Ellis

2.10 Gloria Hamilton

There are no consistent figures, over time, for the age distribution of membership, but it is hardly surprising that the majority of members were between ages thirty-five and fifty-five, at least between 2000 and 2002. Too much cannot be read into a comparison of two consecutive years. But those two years, if taken as indicative, would suggest a decline in the younger age cohort and an increase in the older age cohort of membership, a possible result of emigration.

Table 2.2. Age Structure of Membership

	2000–2001	2001–2002
36 and under	25%	23%
36–45	35%	29%
46–55	24%	29%
56 and over	16%	19%

Source: Annual Reports 2000–2001 and 2001–2002.

Finally, the membership of the Institute, which grew from twenty in 1965 to 241 in 1974 and 311 in 1978, was fundamentally urban in its origins and in its development. Up to 1998, the geographic distribution of membership favoured Kingston and St Andrew with 88 per cent of the membership. In contrast, St James and St Catherine had 3 per cent each, Overseas 4 per cent, Manchester and St Ann 1 per cent each, other parishes zero.[37] The Institute partly compensated by conducting major meetings in Montego Bay, and, over time, establishing examination centres in St James (Montego Bay), St Ann (Moneague) and Manchester (Knox College). In its effort to be as inclusive as possible, the Institute facilitated the involvement of Seventh Day Adventists whose Sabbath precluded them from participation in some of the Institute's activities. Within the first two years of the twenty-first century, the nucleus of a chapter of the ICAJ was established in Montego Bay. The Montego Bay Chapter was formalized during the Bruce Scott regime (2015–17).

Membership of the Institute is partly driven by the desire to further individual professional careers. However, there is, on the other hand, a strong spirit of voluntarism. The fact that so many members of the Institute are also members of the Kiwanis and Rotary service clubs suggests that some members are inspired, at least partly, by the ideal of voluntary public service.

The following chapter examines how the Institute consolidated itself between 1975 and 1989 in the midst of economic crises and political volatility in Jamaica.

Chapter 3

Strengthening the Foundations, 1975–1989

During this period, the Institute sharpened its definition of the organization's general role, raised its national profile and underscored its relevance to the needs of the wider society, which faced a period of economic and political volatility. The Institute successfully stood up to brief challenges to its unity and credibility, strengthened its international ties and established permanent headquarters at 8 Ruthven Road. The promotion of a two-tier system of accountancy, the effort to indigenize the profession as well as the outreach to other English-speaking territories that took place during these years will be discussed in chapters 4 and 5.

Proposals for institutional change emerged partly from peculiar Jamaican circumstances in the 1970s but also from a sense of urgency to foster the growth of the profession. A discussion paper by President D.C. Sale (1976–77) made a number of proposals, some of which were taken up by the Institute. Sale's proposal that the Institute pay closer attention to student complaints and establish closer lines of communication between the student body and the Council inferred that there were issues of contention between the students and the Council. Causes of student frustration stemmed partly from low pass rates, partly from examination room conditions, and sometimes from what they saw as the indifference of the Council to student interests. Large numbers of working students were stagnating at various points in their educational programme. Sale's suggestion of a two-tier system was partly a response to the problems of students but was also driven by the need for a larger body of Jamaican accounting technicians. Sale also proposed an updating of the ethical rules of the Institute to conform more closely to developments abroad. Further proposals included the setting of local examinations, providing full-time courses and reinforcing the principle of continuing (post-qualification) education. Finally, in 1976, Sale recommended that the Institute acquire its own premises, a suggestion that was initially rejected on the grounds of affordability. As president, he was also a strong advocate of cooperation with other English-speaking Caribbean territories.[1]

While Sale's proposals were concerned, fundamentally, with professional training and development, ethics and infrastructure, and a two-tier system, Carroll Thorburn's proposals argued for a less reactive and more innovative approach by the ICAJ to meet the specific needs of Jamaica. Probably influenced by the contentious ideological issues of the day – the era of democratic socialism – Thorburn saw a role for the profession in community development through the promotion of small enterprises. He also identified cane farming and tourist enterprises as areas of the economy that deserved the attention of accountants. He advocated greater interest in legislative matters (including taxation) and their potential effects on the social structure and on national life prior to enactment. He especially targeted state enterprises that had increased in number during the 1970s for the attention of the accounting profession. He also recommended that the Institute should perform an information and advisory function with respect to the recently established National Housing Trust. In a specific reference to the government's programme of "worker participation" that gave workers (through politically generated "mass mobilization") a voice in their workplace, Thorburn argued that worker participation would be better served by enabling workers to purchase shares in the companies that employed them. Finally, he reasserted the original vision of the Institute – reducing Jamaica's reliance on overseas personnel.[2]

At that time, some members of the Institute believed that while the needs of students and the increase in the number of Jamaican accountants were important concerns, they should not be the sole functions of the Institute, which had a larger national function to perform. In a comparable vein, Jasper Burnett issued probably the first blast against Jamaican government financial accounting. The speech, an attack on the auditor general's report, emphasized what Burnett called a "preoccupation with vouchers", the failure to account for "large sums" by various ministries and departments, and the absence of "accountability" on the part of government:

> On broader aspects, it seems that accountability in Government has either been completely broken down or, at best, is treated with scant respect by the persons responsible for the administration of Government finances. . . . It seems ironical that the Private Sector is being compelled to comply with an increasing amount of regulation and red tape . . . while the persons from whom these requirements emanate pay little or no attention to their own accountability. Proper financial accounting is by no means a political football.[3]

The Burnett speech certainly presaged the beginning of consistent efforts by the Institute to monitor and react to government finances, to improve government accounting and auditing procedures, and to introduce more highly trained accountants into government departments. This orientation, voiced in 1978, probably led, in later years, to the formation of a Public Sector and Legislation Review Committee by the Institute. The Institute offered professional advice to the government on the National Housing Trust. It issued a circular (18 March 1977) entitled "Accounting for Employer's Contributions to the National Housing Trust". The ICAJ made several recommendations on how to account for the contribution of employers to the National Housing Trust scheme. In 1975, The ICAJ's Taxation Committee prepared a report on the government's anti-inflation package and offered suggestions on income tax and company law.

The Institute also advised businesses on accounting in the face of significant inflation. These technical services were designed to assist sole practitioners, in particular. A committee of the Institute advised on auditing and accounting matters for all practitioners in Jamaica, whether they were members of the Institute or not. Thus, the Accounting Practice Committee was striving to keep abreast of international pronouncements on accounting practice and at the same time advising on Jamaica's "peculiar needs".[4] The professional advisory services seemed to have gone into abeyance, only to be revived years later, in 1997, to assist small practising firms and sole practitioners in accounting and auditing. There were, therefore, two objectives with which the ICAJ was simultaneously concerned. One was the reform of the accountancy profession itself. The other was the adoption of accounting skills to meet the social and political needs of Jamaica in the mid-1970s.

The Institute played an important role as adviser to businesses on financial reporting and auditing in the context of prolonged inflationary tendencies in Jamaica and overseas. President Alastair MacBeath (1974–76) also reported that, "to date, CMP Industries Ltd. [was] the only Company . . . to provide in its annual report to share-holders (1979) supplementary information disclosing the ravages of inflation upon its performance". Exposure Draft (ED) 24 was one forward step in the "gradual evolution of generally accepted inflation accounting principles".[5] The ICAJ also undertook a review of policies relating to redundancy payments in published accounts. It is difficult to determine the impact of the ICAJ's recommendations on any modifications of redundancy legislation passed in 1974. The statement made by President Vintoria Bernard much later, in 2011, is relevant to what the Institute was attempting to do in the 1970s when she declared: "As accounting professionals, we are engaged in helping businesses to navigate the economic rapids . . . develop new opportunities while exploring new territories."[6] In brief, accountants reacted to circumstances. Dereck Sale reported in 1976 that businesses were experiencing chronic cash-flow problems, bad debts, low inventories and increased capital outflows. Sale's report warned that "unless present trends are reversed in the near future, it appears that business closures including liquidations and receiverships will have exacerbated the situation beyond 1976".[7]

No one doubted the existence of an economic crisis or that there was an acute shortage of foreign exchange with the attendant shortage of raw materials and consumer goods. The post-1973 oil shocks, resulting from the policy of the Organization of Petroleum Exporting Countries (OPEC) to raise petroleum prices, had placed severe strain on non-oil producers, such as Jamaica. The other explanation for Jamaica's economic problems was that some businesses, revolting against the amicable relationship between the democratic socialist government of the People's National Party and socialist Cuba, migrated, and contributed to capital flight. A third, related to the second, was the adverse effect of government policy on business. The business community questioned the establishment of government-based institutions such as the State Trading Corporation, which, in the view of many Jamaican businessmen, intruded on the turf of the private sector, and threatened an overwhelming role of government in the economy. From the business point of view, the private sector, not the government, was the engine of growth.

Doubting that the Jamaica Manufacturers Association had the leadership potential to resist what businesses perceived as the oncoming clouds of communism,[8] the Jamaican business community, inspired by GraceKennedy's Carlton Alexander, established the Private Sector Organisation of Jamaica (PSOJ) in 1976. The PSOJ, anti-communist and pro-business, encouraged a closer association with the Institute. The ICAJ's association with the PSOJ appears to have been somewhat uneasy at first. Some members thought that their views were in danger of being subsumed under the PSOJ umbrella, and that "the Institute as a professional body should be free to give independent advice where this was sought".[9] At a Council meeting in January 1977, the question of continued association with the PSOJ was raised. It was agreed that the ICAJ would *resume* payment of fees to the PSOJ, "but this would not prevent the Institute from giving independent advice".[10] Nevertheless, the relations with the PSOJ improved to the extent that the Institute and the PSOJ became allies in the promotion of the private sector as the principal instrument of Jamaica's economic growth. Jasper Burnett, president of the ICAJ, was elected to the executive of the PSOJ in November 1978. Other presidents have followed his example, and one ICAJ president, Dennis Chung, has also served as CEO of the PSOJ.

In April 1977, an eleven-man PSOJ team, led by Carlton Alexander and including Jasper Burnett, the president of the ICAJ, met with minister of national mobilization, Dr D.K. Duncan, to discuss matters "affecting the harmonious relationship between the public and private sectors". The four-hour meeting, according to the *Gleaner* report, was "frank and open" – a diplomatic phrase for major disagreements. The outcome of the meeting was the decision that dialogue be maintained, a non-contentious term for irreconcilable differences.[11]

The Institute was directly affected by the economic challenges of the period. Foreign Exchange shortages reduced the Institute's capacity to import reading material for students. Inflationary trends not only adversely affected operational costs but also weakened sound financial management. There were operational deficits and deficits in the student training exercises. Some practising firms ceased their contributions to the Students' Training Fund, and "the topping-up arrangement with CAST was scheduled to come to an end June 30, 1978".[12]

The uncertain times took their toll on the ICAJ and the accounting profession in other ways. There were a reported 127 accountants and 544 businessmen migrating in the late 1970s. Uncertain conditions may have affected the Council itself. President Brian Mair suddenly resigned as president, effective 8 December 1977, after serving for under one year. Vice-President Jasper Burnett took over the presidency. Former president of the Institute Alastair MacBeath, Brian Mair (December 1977), I.M. Brown (February 1978), Laura Johnson (February 1978) and H.A. Fullerton (March 1978) resigned from the Council during 1977–78. Five of the twelve members of the Council, who had attended the first meeting of the ICAJ in February 1965, had migrated. Three of the five were expatriates who went off to Fiji, the Isle of Man and Ireland. Two Jamaicans migrated to Canada and the Cayman Islands. Migration occurred sometimes for reasons given as "personal". It is difficult to determine the extent to which migration and resignation took place for personal reasons or because of prevailing concerns about conditions in Jamaica. Given the high level of emigration of professionals in the late 1970s, it is difficult to escape the conclusion that the movement overseas had been encouraged by prevailing conditions in Jamaica.[13]

Care must be taken to avoid the conclusion that the Institute methodically opposed the government. Some members supported the policies of government. Others obviously did not. One member at least (Dereck Sale) was impressed by the democratic socialist ideology of the Michael Manley administration. In an address to US businessmen in West Palm Beach, Florida, on 15 November 1976, Dereck Sale supported Manley's call for a new international economic order "whereby countries like Jamaica might have a better share of the fruits of the earth". Rich countries needed to have their consciences aroused to "stem the tide of revolution which is fast engulfing the countries of the Third World". Sale criticized the US press for exaggerated (and unfavourable) reports on conditions in Jamaica. Sale's comment on the issue of the bauxite levy gave unmitigated support to the policy of the government: "this had been found necessary for the common good. Jamaica had learnt that political independence was meaningless without economic independence and this meant control of the country's national resources".[14]

Other members, such as Burnett, looked with concern at the economy as "the most pervasive and topical aspect of Jamaican life". The government of the 1970s, meanwhile, gave strong moral support to the indigenization of the profession, a factor that is discussed in the ensuing chapter in greater detail.

The mood of the ICAJ, which had been influenced by the straitened economic circumstances of Jamaica in the 1970s, changed with the general elections of 1980, which brought into political office the business-friendly Jamaica Labour Party administration, headed by Prime Minister Edward Seaga. The role of the Institute was now to make a contribution to "economic recovery" and "structural adjustment". The report for 1980–81 by President Kenneth La Cruise was a clear enunciation of the belief that Jamaica was on the road to economic recovery under the new government:

> Jamaica entered the new decade with a carry-over from the seventies of challenging political and economic problems. However, with the change of government which resulted from the October 1980 general elections, it is evident that the political tension has eased, and that the road to economic recovery is now taking shape. Already, the government has renegotiated the loan agreement with the International Monetary Fund. Further, a number of foreign governments and other international lending agencies have signalled their commitment to support the country's bid for economic recovery. . . . It is gratifying to note that the Institute made significant strides through the difficult periods and confidently looks forward to the challenges of the years ahead.[15]

Jamaica's government between 1980 and 1989, most probably aware of the general ideological orientation of the Institute, called upon the latter's expertise and services. The Institute was, indeed, no longer "faceless". It is worth noting that the concept of shareholding by employees, recommended by Thorburn in 1979, was mirrored in the decision of the Minister of Finance and Prime Minister Seaga to broaden shareholding within the National Commercial Bank (NCB). "The plan was for government to control the divestment to prevent any shareholder from owning more than 7.5 per cent of the equity of NCB. Similar divestment of shares took place with respect to Telecommunications of Jamaica (TOJ), the Caribbean Cement Company and some small or moderate entities."[16]

In his autobiography, former prime minister Edward Seaga singled out Richard Downer (a member of the Institute) and a "leading member of one of the top Audit firms" [PriceWaterhouseCoopers] in Jamaica. Downer led the divesting process of the National Commercial Bank: "Richard Downer was widely acclaimed for his work, enabling him to launch a second career as a consultant, lecturing in 16 nations in the Third World and countries emerging from communism, where he was sent by USAID, the World Bank, IFC, and the US Department of Commerce."[17]

The Jamaica Labour Party government (1980–89) mobilized the expertise of the Institute's members to help reverse Jamaica's economic slide of the 1970s. For example, Denis Goldson, a founding member of the Institute, and one of Jamaica's representatives on the inter-government working party for the creation of a Customs Union of the Federal Government of the West Indies (1955–58), oversaw the liquidation of the twenty-six sugar workers' cooperatives at Frome, Monymusk and Bernard Lodge.[18] Oliver Clarke, one of the senior managers of the Gleaner Company, chaired the committee responsible for the divestment of hotels, which had come under government control during the 1970s, not so much because of a desire to nationalize the economy, as to respond to the emigration of panicking hotel entrepreneurs.

Prime Minister Edward Seaga placed accountants on several strategic boards, thereby both symbolically and, in reality, defining the economic/free enterprise focus of his regime: President Kenneth La Cruise was appointed a member of the boards of the Jamaica Broadcasting Corporation (JBC) and of the Jamaica Export Trading Company Ltd; Oliver Clarke, chairman of National Hotels and Properties, was responsible for the divestment of hotels; Henry G Fullerton, member of the Coconut Industry Board; Carlisle Gray, a member of the Tobacco Industry Board; Ivan S. Heron, member of the Public Service Commission; Lloyd James, Board of the *Daily News*; Philmore Ogle, member of the Divestment Committee; L.R. "Lannie" Reynolds, chairman of the Cornwall Regional Hospital Board; Christopher Roberts, Coffee Industry Board; K.L. Robertson, member of the Divestment Committee; Sir Edgerton Richardson, Jamaica's permanent representative to the United Nations. Cecil Harvey became accountant general of Jamaica. Richard Downer oversaw the divestment of National Commercial Bank on behalf of the government.[19]

The ICAJ was obviously pleased with the responsibilities that the new government had placed on it. The president of the ICAJ, Kenneth Lewis, noted in his report (1983–84) that "It is most gratifying to note that the Prime Minister in his Budget speech mentioned the Institute as one of the professional bodies [that] he would be asking for assistance in carrying out his tax reforms."[20] In 1985–86, Aulous Madden reported on the "vital and dynamic role" played by the Institute's Taxation Committee in the government's major tax reform. Aulous Madden declared in a speech to the PSOJ: "The PSOJ represents a group of dedicated companies and private sector associations and individuals who are determined to see Jamaica progress and prosper as a free enterprise economic system, a system which we consider to be the surest means for creating prosperity for the majority of Jamaicans in a democratic environment." While that speech confirmed the Institute's support of government's divestment plans, which were quickly underway, Madden's speeches to the PSOJ, the Jamaica Employers' Federation, his letters to the minister of trade and industry and to the prime minister and minister of finance, and his presentation at the Bar of the House of Representatives, pointing to anomalies and inequities in the government's tax proposals, indicate that the Institute was prepared to question some of the taxation measures.[21]

Divestment policies, rapprochement with the United States, and the IMF were intended to combat Jamaica's economic crisis, which included chronic inflation, devaluation and foreign exchange scarcity. A major thrust was, however, the revision of the onerous and complicated tax code, to which Prime Minister Seaga attributed widespread tax evasion and reduction of government's revenues.

The Tax Structure Examination Project (TSEP) team, led by Professor Roy Bahl of Syracuse University, consisted of "fifty experts, specialists and consultants" from the United States and Jamaica.[22] Members of the ICAJ continued to serve on a Tax Reform (Successor) Committee that made recommendations on personal income tax and in 1986–87 on corporate taxation and general consumption tax (GCT).[23]

Jasper Burnett, however, did not cease his agitation for expanding the number of Jamaican accountants, and to ensure that the ICAJ had an "independent" voice. Indeed, bearing in mind the concentration on economic reconstruction, Jasper Burnett, in an exchange between the PAB and the Council of the Institute in May 1982, pointed out that the "level of financial accountability which is necessary for the restructuring of the economy is simply not in place. The existing accounting manpower cannot effectively address all the critical features necessary for this mammoth task." According to Burnett: "There are now approximately 300 qualified Jamaican Accountants. This gives a ratio of 1:7,000 of the population, compared to 1:500 in the UK. To offset this serious imbalance, accountants have to be recruited from overseas. This is but a short-term answer to a perennial and growing problem." Burnett emphasized that the facilities for training students were far from adequate to meet the demands of "restructuring".[24] The current reality was that students still relied on "practical training" from the professional firms, did correspondence courses, obtained from the United Kingdom, or attended the College of Arts Science and Technology and wrote the ICAJ/ACCA Professional Examinations. The CAST programme admitted twenty-nine students annually. There was an annual intake of some 150 students to the BSc programme and forty to the MSc programme at the UWI, Mona. After paying due credit to accounting firms which allowed students time off, or contributed financially to the training of students, Burnett noted that government in its PAA had remained silent with respect to financing the ICAJ. He referred to the high cost of recruiting expatriates and the inability of many organizations to afford expatriate personnel; the increasing difficulty of attracting and retaining expatriate personnel; high expatriate turnover; and foreign exchange expenditure incurred in expatriate employment. He recommended that the PAB and the Council of ICAJ jointly approach the minister of industry and commerce, Douglas Vaz, and Prime Minister Seaga in his capacity as minister of finance to request that the PAB be recognized under the HEART programme as a training body; that the Ministry of Finance allocate not less than $750,000 per annum out of the HEART Fund to meet the cost of training; that the PAB be given authority to engage the ICAJ as a training institution, thus enabling the PAB to fund the training programme.

The case for increasing the numbers of accountants was strengthened by the situation in the public service. In 1983, of 449 positions in the Income Tax Department there were 150 mostly technical vacancies. Low salaries in the public service contributed to the shortage of accountants in the public service.[25] The Government of Jamaica consulted the Institute on the provision of expertise in the public sector, which was short of qualified and efficient accountants. In 1981, Minister Vaz specifically referred to the shortage of accountants in the government service and to the possibility of contracting private audit firms to assist in accrediting public accounts, in order to relieve pressures in the Auditor General's Department.[26]

National and International Consolidation

In the midst of the various challenges in the 1970s, the Institute had consolidated its international relations and the challenge to the Institute's credibility. In Munich, at the Eleventh International Congress of Accountants in October 1977, the Institute, through its president, Gerald Mair, signed up as a founding member of the International Federation of Accountants (IFAC). Membership of IFAC may be viewed as an international extension of the ICAJ's link with the ACCA since the latter was also a founding member of the new international federation. The IFAC was central to the efforts after the 1970s to harmonize accountancy procedures at the international level. Its influence has grown in proportion to the increasing demand for the methodical formulation of international standards in accountancy. The International Federation of Accountants has become one of the most powerful international accounting bodies. By 1981, IFAC's membership included seventy-six accountancy bodies from fifty-eight countries.

3.1 Brian Mair, 1977 (Mair's presidency lasted just a few months in 1977)

The ICAJ also holds membership in the (IASC), which was established in 1973 with a mandate to "improve and harmonize global accounting standards".[27] The International Accounting Standards Committee's membership included sixty-one accounting bodies from forty-seven countries. Given the overlap of function between the IFAC and the IASC, there was an attempted merger in the 1970s.[28] The Institute also maintained relationships with the Institute of Chartered Accountants of England and Wales (ICAEW), and the Institute of Chartered Accountants of Scotland (ICAS).

Local Challenges to the Institute

Although by 1975 the ICAJ seemed well established as an institution, it had to defend itself, in the late 1970s, against occasional challenges to its legitimacy, unity and performance. There was dissatisfaction in some quarters with the pace at which Jamaicans were replacing expatriate accountants ten years after the Institute's foundation.

The regulations of the Institute and of the PAB ensured that the Institute would zealously guard the right to use the term "chartered" which was, in law, the exclusive right of the Institute. The Institute took legal action against "The Chartered Institute of Public Accountants". Advertisements in the press announcing the formation of this new body during November 1978 created a high level of "confusion". To resolve the issue, the Council took legal action against Vincent Stafford and others in April 1979.[29] Stafford, chairman of the Unification of the Accounting Profession in Jamaica and the main figure behind the Chartered Institute of Public Accountants, clearly did not believe that the profession had been unified, at least not to his satisfaction.[30]

Those who had petitioned for the formation of the new chartered body withdrew the petition in February 1979. One of the persons withdrawing from the petition was Paul A. Desnoes (FAIA) who later became president of the Institute.[31] The ICAJ did not go unchallenged in other respects. Twelve years after the foundation of the Institute, Mr J.J. Jolly, chairman of the Jamaican District Society of the Association of International Accountants Ltd revived strong anti-expatriate sentiments. Jolly argued, in a December 1975 letter to the *Gleaner's* editor, that

1. Jamaica had become the "dumping ground" for expatriate accountants.
2. The continued use of expatriate accountants in management positions was *diametrically opposed to the new social order of Jamaica* [italics added].
3. The importation of foreign accountants did not redound to Jamaican interests.
4. The shortage of accountants in multi-national audit firms is apparent because they are not making their working conditions and promotion of opportunities attractive to Jamaican accountants, and consequently even after joining these firms they become frustrated and move out to industry.
5. Expatriates were available for employment in Jamaica because supply exceeded demand in their country of origin. They also earned more in Jamaica than at home, particularly if they found employment in the multinational firms.
6. Some of the jobs done by the expatriates could be done by Jamaicans.
7. A more rigorous enforcement of the Work Permit Law was needed.[32]

Jolly's approach reflected the 1970s version of nationalism in Jamaica. His assertion that the continued use of expatriate accountants was "diametrically opposed to the new social order of Jamaica" indicates a relationship between his views and those of the ruling government. Indeed, it appears that the relevant minister supported the AIA's position.

The response of J.D. Liddle (a practising accountant) to Mr Jolly four days later was predictable: that expatriates were doing a good job filling the vacancies in the profession. Those vacancies were likely to continue for a few more years. Jolly's request for a more rigorous implementation of the work permit law was therefore uncalled for, as far as Liddle was concerned. He challenged Jolly to support his argument with facts and figures.

Jolly did not present the "facts and figures". But the "facts and figures" supported both Jolly's and Liddle's positions. The output of graduates was not nearly enough to fill the three hundred potential vacancies if all expatriates left the island.[33] Passes in the professional examinations between 1978 and 1982 were not encouraging. (See table 3.1.)

Table 3.1. Professional Passes, 1978–1982

	Total	**1982**	**1981**	**1980**	**1979**	**1978**
ICAJ/ACCA	40	5	5	13	11	6
MSc (Acc)	55	12	15	11	7	10
Total	95	17	20	24	18	16
Annual Av.	19					

Source: Margaret Mendes, "An Examination of Jamaica's Accountancy Training Problems (Part 1)" (September 1983), 6: table 3.

The figures for the period 1975–1981 averaged only fourteen per annum with lows of six in 1978 and five in 1981.[34]

The most vibrant attack on Jolly's views came from Philmore Ogle. Jolly's argument that Jamaican accountants were not being employed was not true, claimed Ogle. There was no shortage of jobs for Jamaican accountants. The suggestion that Jamaican accountants left the larger firms because of a lack of incentive to remain in their employment overlooked the reality that they left the firms for more promising remuneration in industry and commerce.

The eight large firms, subject to attack from Jolly, as serving "foreign interests", were in fact partnerships between local and international institutions, which facilitated international clients. Furthermore, the large firms were the ones whose expertise, assistance to students and financial contributions had ensured that the Jamaican accountancy profession remained afloat.[35]

The true origins of the impasse were the ambitions of the Association of International Accountants (AIA), which had been excluded from membership of the ICAJ, because their membership was not considered to be in "the public interest". In the face of a softening of then minister of industry and commerce Vivian Blake, and of the PAB towards the AIA, Ogle went on the warpath, going so far as to suggest a restructuring of the PAB.[36]

However, the Institute, for the time being, made efforts to expand the number of accounting students especially through the UWI and CAST. The UWI MSc in accounting, which we discuss in the following chapter, was one avenue that the Institute hoped to use to augment the number of Jamaican accountants. It is also relevant to note that, in the post-1975 period, the ICAJ expanded the accounting fraternity by introducing a second tier of accountancy in the island, a sure indication that the ICAJ had not been inactive.

New Headquarters

Given the prevailing circumstances in Jamaica in the late 1970s, it is a source of wonder that the ICAJ was able to finance and establish its own headquarters in 1980. The modest beginnings of the Institute in 1965 dictated that councillors meet in the offices of William Thwaites (1965–68) on Duke Street, and then the home of the secretary, Mrs Sybil Dunkerly, on Old Hope Road, and subsequently the office of Mr R.V. Irvine, the auditor general and acting executive director of the Institute. The Council then moved on 16 April 1974 to their own offices at 75 Half-Way-Tree Road, which they leased from the Victoria Mutual Building Society for three years. The transfer of offices to 45 Duke Street during the last week of July 1978 provided a general office, a council room, a library and three other offices to house the secretariat, which, at the time, consisted of one temporary and four permanent employees. There was parking space for only twelve motor vehicles.

3.2 Original headquarters of ICAJ, 1980

Proposals made from at least 1976 that the ICAJ establish its own headquarters had been rejected on the grounds of affordability. The lease of Duke Street was due to expire in June 1980. The offer of the landlord to sell the Duke Street building to the ICAJ for $100,000 was rejected – again on the grounds of affordability.[37] There were other objections. Apart from inadequate parking space, there was the pressure to follow the broad migratory movement of businesses from "downtown" Kingston to more central sites "uptown".[38] The urgency of identifying alternative accommodation was hastened by the decision of the new landlord to raise the rental to $800 per month. This, again, was considered by some members to be beyond the means of the Institute.

These events forced the Jasper Burnet–led Council (1977–1980) to put on the agenda the purchase of the Institute's own headquarters with greater accessibility for members and students. The Council appointed a committee chaired by Vice-President Kenneth La Cruise to scout for suitable premises for purchase.[39] In 1980, La Cruise identified and recommended a 28,000 square foot property at 8 Ruthven Road valued at $70,000 as suitable accommodation for the new headquarters. The property was considered central and accessible. La Cruise, having persuaded the vendors to accept an offer of $66,000, deposited 10 per cent.[40] Legal fees and renovations over three months were estimated at $30,000. The Ruthven Road site, cleared of its mango trees, provided room for significant expansion.

Some members of the Council objected. It can be readily understood why there was some scepticism in Council. The purchase and preparation costs approached the $100,000 that the Council had rejected for the Duke Street property on the grounds of affordability. Two council members strenuously protested that the cost was beyond the Institute's resources, that the building was unsuitable and the acquisition process had been too secretive.[41] The dissidents recommended that the deposit be written off. One member, Norman M. Adam, felt sufficiently strongly about the matter to write his resignation (later withdrawn). Nevertheless, the Council overwhelmingly ratified the purchase by a vote of nine to two.

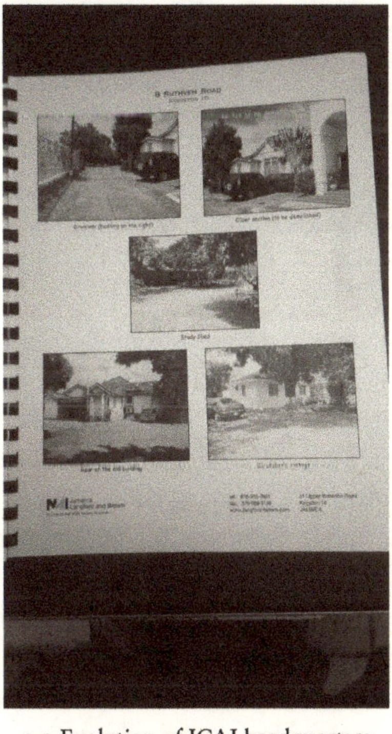

3.3 Evolution of ICAJ headquarters

Even the progressive Thorburn, in one of a flurry of letters to the ICAJ Council, commented on the dubious economics of purchasing new headquarters. "It therefore appears that owning our own premises – with possibly no additional space advantage – is now costing an extra $8,410 per annum." Nor was Thorburn happy with the apparent merger of private funds (coming from two members) to "guarantee" the mortgage. "The principle," he argued, "was incorrect."[42]

3.4 Headquarters in transition

There were also objections to the way the purchase was financed – there was no provision for the use of funds from the student fund, as had been planned by the executive. The agreement was that funds from the student training fund and from the ICAJ itself ($48,000) would be on a loan basis. The ICAJ received a mortgage of $38,844 from the Jamaica National Building Society thanks to Managing Director Lancelot Reynolds of the Jamaica National Building Society (JNBS).[43] La Cruise, no doubt using his leverage with A.Z. Preston, to whom he reported (but also a long-time acquaintance) at UWI's Bursary and who was chairman of the PAB, identified another loan of $17,000 from the PAB at 10 per cent for eight years, with a three-year moratorium. Loans totalling $27,500 were also obtained from firms, with $16,000 received and $11,500 in pledges. President Burnett urged members to contribute more in order to make up the deficit with the issue of another debenture which would be repayable over three years (1981–84). The shortfall was met by funds available at the ICAJ, primarily those for the Student Training Fund, the Education Fund and the funds raised from the *Charter* magazine, which was first published in 1979. Contributions from members ensured the financial viability of the project.

La Cruise became president in July 1980 and was, therefore, the first president of the ICAJ to occupy the new premises. New estimates were now $105,842, plus estimates for the extension of the library and the reading room, which brought the total to $110,842. Price Waterhouse in a letter to La Cruise stated that it would have no objections if its contributions to the Student Training Scheme were utilized by the ICAJ to meet the expenses of acquisition, repairs and maintenance. Price Waterhouse agreed that the funds from the Student Training Fund were to be advanced to the Institute in the form of an interest-free debenture. The use of the funds from the Student Training Scheme to finance the acquisition, repair and refurbishing of the premises was considered somewhat controversial because there was no mention in the by-laws regarding the borrowing powers of the Council.

3.5 Kenneth La Cruise, 1980–81, who was active, on behalf of the Council, in the identification and refurbishing of ICAJ headquarters in 1980

Although the overall credit must be given to the Jasper Burnett–led Council, and the moral support given by Burnett himself, the importance of the footwork of Kenneth La Cruise and his committee cannot be denied. The reconstruction and refurbishment of headquarters have been continuous, facilitated by building committees and the enthusiasm of succeeding presidents.

Summary

The foundation and growth of the ICAJ between 1965 and 1988 was a response to the shortage of Jamaican accountants. There were also nationalistic considerations on the part of some energetic leaders of Jamaican accounting firms. During those years, the accountancy profession achieved some degree of unity, the statutory fundamentals of the Institute were laid, and permanent headquarters established at 8 Ruthven Road. Internationally, the Institute joined the International Accounting Standards Committee (IASC) and IFAC. The relationship with the rest of the English-speaking Caribbean was still fledgling but was under discussion. The Institute had weathered the cross-winds of Jamaican politics and economy since the mid-1970s. During this time, the Institute made a very clear decision that it would no longer be a "faceless" society. It would be not only "reactive" but innovative as well. Over the period 1965 to 1988, the membership of the Institute had grown from the original twenty to 440 in 1988.

While recalling the year 1977–78 as significant for the ICAJ, President Jasper Burnett spoke, with justifiable pride, of the "great strides" made both on the local as well as the regional and international scene by the Institute. The ICAJ, he argued, had continued to grow in stature, and most objectives had been achieved. The point was that the ICAJ had done quite well under the volatile political and economic conditions in Jamaica in the later 1970s. The challenges to the hegemony and legitimacy of the ICAJ had been met through legal intervention. The challenges of the 1980s had also been overcome. The period after 1980 shows the beginning of a partnership with government in economic and financial reform. During the 1980s, indigenization received some setbacks, as we will see in the following two chapters. However, the two-tier system grew and expanded the student body. The following two chapters examine the efforts of the ICAJ to establish an indigenous Jamaican profession, in association with other Caribbean institutes.

Chapter 4

Indigenization

Indigenization is a major and constant theme in the first twenty years of the Institute. Contributing to the indigenization process were the introduction of a BSc (Econ) with Accounting at UWI in 1967; a two-tier system of preparation for accountancy; and an MSc in Accounting at UWI in 1975. The close alliance between the Institute and the ACCA in these early years did not contradict the mission to establish an "indigenous" profession, insofar as the localizers viewed their association with the ACCA as transitional. A 1968 report declared that the intention was to make the accounting profession "truly Jamaican". Members in favour of indigenization were concerned both with increasing the Jamaican accounting body and with establishing an accountancy profession that mirrored the Jamaican environment.

Uriel Salmon (president 1971 to 1973), like other localizers, believed that a Jamaican accountancy profession should mirror Jamaica's environment. In 1973, at the Eighth Annual General Meeting of the Institute, Salmon recommended that Jamaica set its own examinations "beginning with Jamaican Company Law and Income Tax papers".[1] The challenge then, and for the next four decades, was that such courses required "appropriate text books". The discussion of the issue of Jamaican-based (or Caribbean-based) examinations in those two subjects has continued into the twenty-first century.

It was expected that the ICAJ/ACCA partnership would extend over a two- or three-year period, at the end of which time the Mona campus of the UWI would become responsible for the Institute's examinations. Not all members of the ICAJ favoured indigenization. There were "internationalists" who preferred to have ACCA continue beyond three years. However, indigenization had been at the root of the Institute's policy from May 1965 (four months following the foundation of the ICAJ) and was encouraged by the assumption that the relationship between the ICAJ and the ACCA would be phased out after three years. The UWI route was intended to be the "indigenous" route to membership of the ICAJ. An additional incentive to indigenization was a fresh effort in 1968 to integrate the UK accounting bodies, in order to exercise some control over the proliferation of accounting bodies in the UK. Integration would have led to the termination of ACCA examinations in Jamaica.[2] Philmore Ogle (president 1968–70) recommended December 1971 as the starting date for indigenous examinations.[3] The argument for indigenization was, in part, sentimental. But, insofar as there was an association between indigenization and the developmental needs and interests of Jamaica, there were nationalist considerations. However, it proved easier in the medium term to sell the idea of increasing the number of Jamaican accountants based on British models in syllabuses and examinations than to effect qualitative changes needed to indigenize the profession.

Given that the tertiary institutions of UWI and CAST were the natural academic locations for indigenization, the ICAJ supported the accounting programmes at UWI and at CAST in three main ways. First, the Institute offered financial assistance to UWI, which initiated its BSc (Economics) with Accounting in 1967. The Institute, through Carroll Thorburn and Philmore Ogle, raised funds from accounting firms and from other private sector interests to finance, for five years, a lectureship in accountancy at UWI. With respect to CAST, the Institute persuaded professional firms in Jamaica to contribute approximately $30,000 per annum to the Institute's fund to supplement salaries paid by CAST to lecturers teaching courses in accountancy. Through this topping up process, CAST was able to attract more suitably qualified lecturers for its accounting programme.[4] Second, members of the Institute offered their teaching services. Philmore Ogle was one of the first lecturers in the UWI Accounting course, and Denis Goldson acted as an examiner in auditing. Third, the Institute ensured that graduates of the BSc programme would receive exemptions from some ACCA examinations. With the introduction of the BSc (with accounting) at UWI, the latter's extramural accounting programme was transferred to CAST. The CAST Diploma in Business Administration, together with the accounting option, and the UWI's BSc were, then, the bases for the creation of a Jamaican, home-grown accountancy profession.

The idea of introducing an MSc (Accounting) at UWI, Mona, the brainchild of Philmore Ogle, was supported by the ACCA – at first. The MSc was first taught in 1975. The collapse of the British integration scheme in August 1970 did not sway the ICAJ from its goal of conducting local examinations. The ACCA resumed its partnerships in the Caribbean, and, in fact, made its own contribution to the formulation of the UWI MSc (Accounting) programme. The partnership of ICAJ and ACCA was strengthened by the introduction of the Association of Accounting Technicians (AAT) in 1979 and eventually the Certified Accounting Technician (CAT) certification in 1997.

Another incentive to promote indigenization came from the Government of Jamaica during the 1970s.

Government Support of Indigenization.

Minister of trade, industry and tourism Robert Lightbourne had championed the formation of the Institute in the 1960s. In the 1970s, however, the approach of government to accountancy and the Institute reflected a more radical orientation that strongly favoured complete autonomy for Jamaican accountancy. It may be argued, however, that the search for autonomy of the accountancy profession by government proved more rhetorical than substantial.

In the mid-1970s, the Ministry of Industry and Commerce, under whose portfolio the Institute fell, showed impatience with the Institute, accusing it of delaying the development of an autonomous local accountancy profession.[5] Although, the minister argued, "one of the functions of the Institute is to make provision for the training, education and examination of persons engaging in or intending to take up the accounting profession, now six years after its incorporation, the Institute can give no assurance that local examinations geared to meet Jamaica's needs will be established by 1980, and it is clear that it cannot be regarded as adequately discharging its responsibility in this matter."[6] The Ministry of Industry and Commerce insisted that "localization" of examinations was a "must", "not only from the foreign exchange point of view, but from the aspect of training our people in such a manner that they can deal with the particular problems in our Jamaican situation".[7]

In 1978, a year later, the minister addressed, favourably, the issue of localization, with a focus this time on mid-level accountants. The ministry, the PAB and CAST were "working toward replacing these [ACCA] examinations with local examinations which can be hallmarks of achievement as junior qualifications and which will facilitate the movement from bookkeeping to mid-level accounting persons and ultimately to the qualified accountant". He urged the Institute to "press towards a Jamaican examination by 1980 which will qualify entrants for admission to the ICAJ".[8]

The government (1972–80) then demonstrated an interest in "localization" of the profession in the 1970s. It also endorsed the three major initiatives of the nationalists: to phase out the ACCA by 1980–81, to increase the number of accountants and to introduce a two-tier system of accountancy qualifications. The government, much less enthusiastic about financing the work of the Institute, ruled (through the attorney general) against a proposal by the ICAJ in association with CAST to establish an Accountancy Training Foundation to identify adequate funds for the training of accountants. The suggestion that the government itself assist with financing the expansion of accountancy was coldly received by the minister.[9]

Two Tiers

One of the most important developments in the 1970s was the establishment and consolidation of a two-tier system in the accountancy profession. The first steps in the establishment of a two-tier system actually came with the BSc (Economics) with Accounting (1967) and the CAST Diploma in Business, Accounting option. However, the ACCA/ICAJ also promoted a two-tier system parallel to the programmes at CAST and UWI. The ACCA/ICAJ's two tiers began with the introduction of the Institute of Accounting Staff (IAS), which was succeeded by the AAT in 1981. The Institute, starting in 1976, initiated discussions on a "two-tier" system to train a larger cadre of accounting technicians. The case for a two-tier system was presented by D.C. Sale as follows:

- More graduates were needed in industry, commerce and government.
- Students were looking for "easier qualifications" because the ACCA course often led to frustration.
- No official recognition was given to employees in industry, commerce and government who through experience alone had attained certain

levels of proficiency but who had no academic professional qualification. No encouragement was given unless they aspired to the position of chartered accountants.

- It would be unwise to lower the standards of the Institute of Chartered Accountants of Jamaica.
- The ICAJ was, perhaps, too preoccupied with qualification at the highest professional level to give attention to the need for upgrading skills at the level of technician. As a developing country, Jamaica needed non-professional accounting staff.[10]

4.1 Dereck Sale, 1976–77, advocate of a system for preparing accounting technicians and of a Caribbean apex body of accountants

Having made the case, Sale proposed:

- A second-tier institute to be called the Institute of Accounting Staff of Jamaica (IAS), which would be incorporated into the Public Accountancy Act. The new institute would cater exclusively to non-practising accountants and would have as its founding members senior accounting personnel in industry, commerce and government who have a prescribed amount of experience, and persons who hold certain qualifications or certificates, or a combination of both.
- The institute would be attached to the PAB.
- Examination papers would be set by the ICAJ, preferably through the Institute of Accounting Staff (IAS) in the UK.
- The proposal also allowed for exemptions on the road to ICAJ membership. The programme would reduce the tendency for loose use of the term "accountant" in Jamaica.

4.2 Jasper Burnett (president, 1977–80), who took over as president following the sudden resignation of Brian Mair, strongly advocated the two-tier system, the indigenization of the profession, the acquisition of ICAJ's own headquarters, and a Caribbean apex body of accountants.

In 1978, Jasper Burnett, speaking on behalf of the Institute, endorsed the concept of the two-tiered system. (The first tier would be the chartered accountants, and the second tier would be holders of an ICAJ diploma in accounting en route, if desired, towards ICAJ/ACCA certification.) The two-tier idea had the support of the minister of industry and commerce, who also undertook to seek financial assistance for the expansion of the relevant faculties at UWI and CAST.[11]

The result of the negotiations was not the establishment of a second-tier Institute as envisaged by Dereck Sale, but the adoption by the Institute of the ACCA's Accounting Staff (IAS) and a few years later the Association of Accounting Technicians (AAT). The ICAJ was the first overseas agency to embrace the AAT. The first examination of the Institute of Accounting Staff was proctored by the Overseas Examinations Committee in December 1975. In 1979–80 some 129 and in 1980–1981 some 145 students received admission to the IAS/AAT.[12]

The College of Arts, Science and Technology (CAST – successor to the Institute of Technology) proved to be one of the strongest advocates of a two-tier system of "localization" or a "national qualification" in accountancy. The CAST programme would cater to persons who did "accountancy work" at lower levels of an enterprise but who were not adequately trained, and who would never, by reason of their limited educational background, qualify to enter the ACCA programme. Such students would not expect membership of the ICAJ. The CAST qualification would be acceptable in Jamaica through the Institute at the technological level. The programme would also conform to international standards to give full exposure to graduates who would quite likely have to engage with transnational companies. CAST urged the ICAJ to recognize the CAST qualification as a second-tier qualification. CAST also wished (with the support of the ICAJ) to launch the programme without waiting for prior accreditation from the ACCA, given the urgent need for such training. Finally, while holders of the CAST qualification would not expect membership of the ICAJ, it was expected that members of the ICAJ would employ such graduates. Noting that financial assistance to CAST had ended when the ICAJ opted to employ a director of studies (UWI/ICAJ) rather than top up the salaries of CAST lecturers, the CAST president, Dr Alfred Sangster, recommended the "establishment of a fund for the sole purpose of training accountants".[13]

In April 1978, the Council accepted that holders of the CAST Diploma in Accounting would be eligible for entry into Tier 2. CAST not only had the ardent support of its innovative principal, but also of government, which accepted the principle of second-tier examinations. Earlier, in March 1978, the Council reported that CAST "had had discussions with the Minister and with the PAB with a view of arriving at a consensus on proposals for the localization of examinations and distance teaching". The meeting also, significantly, agreed to "give further consideration to the phasing out of the ACCA examination by 1980–81".[14] The PAB, at a joint meeting of ICAJ, the PAB and minister of industry and commerce R.D. Williams on 13 November 1978, accepted the proposal to establish a two-tier system: "The PAB and CAST [are] working toward replacing these examinations with local examinations which can be hallmarks of achievement as junior qualifications and which will facilitate the movement from book-keeping to mid-level accounting persons and ultimately to the qualified accountant."[15]

Developments at CAST created some uneasiness in the Students' Committee of the ICAJ. A memorandum submitted to the Council by Carl W. Gray, chairman of that committee, in January 1978 showed concern about the reduction of the regulatory powers of the Institute over CAST in terms of staff selection and examinations. The main concern seems to have been that the ICAJ could lose all leverage or control over CAST. The main points of the memorandum were:

- A CAST education could be received at moderate cost.
- The government was willing to support CAST, if it believed it politic to do so, even to the "detriment of the ICAJ".
- By withdrawing financial support, the ICAJ had lost its leverage over CAST. The Council was unable to *control* the CAST programme.
- The Institute was unable to determine what was happening at CAST insofar as that institution was succeeding in gaining its own overseas accreditation, especially with respect to supervisory functions and accounting technicians.
- CAST was extending its teaching into rural Jamaica. The institution was already working on cooperation with the community colleges (community colleges had been established since 1974) to offer

accountancy training under CAST's supervision in rural communities. Colleges selected were Mount Alvernia, Excelsior and Knox colleges.

- With the preference of the government of the day for localization of syllabuses, CAST was in a strong position vis-à-vis government. In contrast to UWI and CAST, which had a teaching faculty, the Institute was dependent on accounting and auditing firms to provide teachers of accounting.
- The Institute did not itself have the manpower to conduct full-time training, did not operate a training establishment, and was plagued by financial problems.
- CAST and ICAJ were in competition. . . . The ICAJ will be faced with a situation where the community is happy with an accreditation granted by CAST in direct competition with the Institute's examinations, or even preference to the Institute's.
- CAST had shown its ability to obtain overseas accreditation. CAST had already done so for the banking diploma and expected to receive accreditation from the Institute of Accounting Staff (England) for permission to offer and mark examinations at Foundations A and B and the Diploma of the Institute of Accounting Staff, respectively.

Sensing that if the Institute took an aloof posture, it would have little or no control over the quality and extension of the CAST programme, and that CAST appeared to be developing a comparative advantage in the training of supervisory and middle-management personnel "for Jamaican needs", the memorandum's recommendations confined itself to the maintenance of continuous and serious dialogue with CAST and to work closely with the institution in the conduct of workshops. The Institute, secondly, should encourage localization with respect to the foundation examinations of the ACA and the Diploma of Accounting Staff.[16]

The outcome of some of these concerns appears to have been (in 1978–79) that, at the invitation of CAST, two members of the Council served on the Advisory Committee for Accountancy Education. ICAJ has also partly funded lectureships at both institutions and consistently provided scholarships and bursaries for accounting students. The Council fully supported the efforts of both CAST and UWI to improve the level of accountancy education and increase the number of graduates.[17] In 1979–80, after discussions with the private sector, CAST, UWI and the PAB proposed that the total output of qualified accountants should not be fewer than fifty persons annually for at least the ensuing five years.[18]

BSc University of the West Indies

The example quoted to justify the development of a locally trained accountancy profession in Jamaica was the successful establishment of the medical and law faculties at the University of the West Indies (UWI). It had been to the UWI that the ICAJ had first turned for assistance in the training of more accountants in Jamaica. The relationship between the UWI, Mona campus, and the ICAJ was driven at first by both the urgency to produce more graduates in accounting in Jamaica and also by a commitment among some "nationalists" to local examinations. Expansion of facilities at the UWI and at CAST was directed towards that end. The BSc (Economics with Accounting) degree was introduced in 1967 within the Department of Management Studies of the Faculty of Social Sciences of the UWI. The BSc succeeded earlier efforts to deploy the resources of the Extra-Mural Department of UCWI (as it was then) to introduce courses in accountancy in Jamaica. The BSc (with Accounting) degree increased the supply of qualified persons to fill middle-level positions where accounting skills were required in industry and commerce, finance, central government and in the accounting profession.[19]

MSc Accounting Degree, University of the West Indies

The MSc became, after its foundation in 1975, an important alternative route to Institute membership and was a key factor in the localization process. The Institute, having encouraged the formulation of the BSc in 1967, gave strong support for the establishment of an MSc (Accounting) at UWI, Mona, in 1975. Even more than the BSc, the graduates of the MSc course were expected (at least by some members of the Institute) to become the major source of chartered accountants in Jamaica. The ACCA contributed its expertise to the formulation of the MSc, its intended replacement. Burnett (1977–80) was particularly keen to link the MSc programme with the phasing out of the ACCA. "The ICAJ considers that it will be necessary to continue examination arrangements with the Association of Certified Accountants of the UK for *a transitional period* [italics added], as the Institute is pursuing discussions with UWI for further expansion of the MSc as the main educational medium for training future chartered accountants."[20]

The BSc degree was a stepping stone leading to the MSc (Accounting) degree. The MSc, a UWI Department of Management Studies programme, had a duration of fifteen months, followed by two years' practical experience in a firm of chartered accountants.[21] The completion of the period of practical working experience entitled graduates to apply directly for membership of the ICAJ. In 1975, there were discussions between ACCA's president, Harry Hill, and Frank Osborne, ACCA's overseas relations secretary, on the one hand, and UWI vice-chancellor A.Z. Preston on the other.[22] The MSc was intended to provide academic training in accounting up to professional level. Normally, to enter the master's programme, students were required to have a first degree in accounting or in management studies with appropriate qualifications in accounting, auditing, management accounting, taxation, executorships, insolvency and trusteeship, project evaluation and financial management, quantitative business analysis and computer applications. In keeping with the commitment to ensure the professional credentials of the MSc, members of UWI's Management Studies faculty served on the ICAJ executive and generally tried (not always successfully) to maintain a cooperative relationship with the professional accounting associations in the Caribbean. The ACCA provided an external examiner for the MSc.

The MSc was advertised in 1976 as the "first time that a local degree will be acceptable to the Council as a qualifying examination".[23] The BSc, apart from its significance as a second-tier accounting programme, functioned as a prerequisite for entry into the MSc and had the effect of improving the pass rate in the post-graduate course. UWI viewed its BSc and MSc programmes as bringing to accountancy not only teaching and professional service but also research and publication in matters of relevance to the profession.

In 1985, Vice-Chancellor Preston of the UWI argued that accountancy was coming to be viewed as a "legitimate academic discipline" with its "own logic and coherence".[24] Preston believed that accountancy education at the university level brought distinct advantages. First, by avoiding narrow skills training, it would broaden and deepen the preparation of the accountant for professional life, beyond auditing and financial reporting. Second, the

UWI was "equipped to give the kind of education which an institution concerned largely with narrower specific professional skills-training alone cannot give". Third, he linked tertiary education with the broader question of the development of Jamaica.[25] Fourth, he argued, the dichotomy between a university-trained accountant and a professional coming through professional bodies was "artificial". He envisaged continued cooperation between ICAJ and the UWI. Later he confided to Alister McIntyre his intention to establish a business school at Mona.[26] In similar vein, Margaret Mendes wrote, "When a profession progresses from the apprenticeship model to academic mode, with this goes the development of the research tradition prompted by the university environment."[27] Both authors mentioned above were convinced that universities could play a positive role in the development of accountancy.

The enthusiasm and optimism that the Institute had for the relationship between the UWI MSc and an indigenized accountancy can be deduced from the following statement made by the Institute in 1978: "The ICAJ feels that its association with ACCA will continue for some time to come but that this will be in effect a transitional period as it is felt that the MSc will take over as the main training ground for the first tier. The University is expected to expand in due course and to include evening and part-time programmes."[28] The confidence in the MSc programme was enhanced by support from accounting firms that offered awards to students of Accountancy.[29]

The continuing collaboration between the UWI and the Institute was confirmed in correspondence between the Institute's president, Dereck Sale, and A.Z. Preston. Sale stated, "As you know the Council has accepted this degree as a qualifying examination for membership of the Institute. . . . At the present time several members of the ICAJ are assisting with the MSc programme, which is going well." Sale very specifically pointed to the challenge that so many students had in their pursuit of an ACCA by correspondence courses and other self-help methods which were "less than satisfactory".[30]

Vice-Chancellor Preston, in turn, acknowledged the assistance of the Institute in providing $8,000 per annum for a part-time lectureship at Mona and confirmed that "arrangements could be made for firms, companies or individuals contributing to the scheme through your body, to benefit from Income Tax exemption on contributions made for the use of the UWI".[31] The Institute, in response, established an educational trust to facilitate individuals and organizations to make tax-free contributions to the Institute through the trust, which would have full responsibility for all educational activities.[32]

The UWI graduated its first seventeen MSc accountancy students in 1976. The first two MSc graduates enrolled as members of the Institute in 1977. Between 1976 and 1982, MSc accountancy graduates numbered seventy-seven or an average of twelve per year. In April 1983, thirty-one MSc graduates (9 per cent) were included in the total ICAJ membership of 352. An average of forty students entered for the MSc and about 150 for the BSc. The MSc seemed destined to become the primary local professional qualification route – a victory for the nationalists. The MSc promised to become, apart from the ACCA certification, the most important local qualification for membership of the Institute and chartered accountancy.

Cooperation between the ICAJ and UWI was advanced in 1978 by the appointment of a director of studies, whose salary was to be shared with the Institute. Underlying the decision to appoint a director of studies was the determination to raise the performance of candidates by improving the quality of tuition for the Institute's and UWI's students, thereby increasing the number of qualified accountants. The duties of the director of studies included part-time lecturing in the MSc course and organizing seminars and pre-examination workshops for non-university students of the Institute, "especially during the transitional period".[33] He was to serve as liaison officer between the UWI and the Institute and act as a general counsellor to students.

Given the discouraging pass rate in the ACCA examinations, the ICAJ turned its attention to the general improvement of student performance by conducting seminars and quarterly lectures on themes of interest to students preparing for their Foundation and professional examinations on behalf of the Student Society. The target was fifty graduates per annum.

While Vice-Chancellor Preston had emphasized that accountancy was an academic discipline in its own right, there were members of the ICAJ who viewed professional, not academic, training as paramount. He was already swimming against a rising tide, because there was evidence from 1976 that segments of the ICAJ were less than satisfied with the MSc route to membership. In that year, there was a complaint in the ranks of the Institute that there was poor communication between the MSc students and lecturers on the one hand and the Institute on the other. President Alastair MacBeath complained that the Institute had not been officially informed of the number of lecturers at UWI and, more seriously, recommended in June 1976 that MSc students should "be brought within the ambit of the Institute's student body".[34]

The dissatisfaction, which really hinged on the ability or inability of the ICAJ to control the programmes of the tertiary institutions, deepened between 1977 and 1988. The ICAJ's negative conclusions about the MSc were buttressed by employers who argued that the MSc route did not demonstrate professional quality. The ACCA, having reassessed its exemptions policy, proposed, from as early as June 1977, the removal of some of the exemptions given to MSc students.[35] The Council also accepted the ACCA's negative conclusions with respect to the theoretical curriculum content of the MSc.[36]

In 1988, the Council, arguing that the MSc did not provide a professional education comparable to that of the ACCA /ICAJ, suspended the MSc programme as a direct entry into the profession, excepting those who had qualified prior to 1986.

Eventually, the new strategy led to the decision in 1986–87 to restrict exemptions previously enjoyed by MSc students to the first two Levels of the ACCA. The insistence that in future MSc students would no longer be exempt from Level III ACCA in effect reduced the MSc to two-thirds of its former value.

The lesson of 1986 to 1987 was that it was the professional body of accountants, not an academic institution, which would thus determine the future of the accounting profession in Jamaica. The official explanation was that the UWI had failed to provide the data requested to determine the level of accreditation to be granted by both bodies for persons who passed the MSc. The result, it was argued, was a double standard in admission policy. Since the MSc was, from the indigenizers' point of view, central to the Jamaicanization (or Caribbeanization) of the profession, the suspension of the MSc qualification amounted to a major reversal of localization.

The suspension of the MSc qualification was strongly supported by veteran accountant and founder of the ICAJ, William Thwaites. The Council, he explained, had "problems with the UWI because the latter had failed to recognize the requirements of a professional body in setting up the MSc Degree".[37] "Academics," he claimed, "found trouble, mental trouble, in accepting the fact that they would have to stay within certain bounds and teach certain things that were required for the professional exams instead of being able to float along on any course that they choose to chart for the degree." Sorting out issues with the UWI took a "long time" and, "as you know today, because they have begun to chart a course which was not to our liking, [the Institute] had to put a temporary stop on using the MSc course as a direct entry into the profession".[38]

The central point made by Thwaites – the influential veteran – was that the UWI had departed too far from the professional requirements of the ACCA/ ICAJ. The impasse between the Institute and the UWI is subject to various interpretations. The work of Owolabi Bakre, whose thesis links the ACCA to post-colonial imperialism and elite collaboration, views the impasse as a conspiracy by the ACCA to secure its turf.[39] Less stridently, Margaret Mendes argues, first, that the MSc and the ACCA were in a "competitive relationship", leading the latter to strive to maintain its premier position. Mendes notes, second, that the MSc "came under pressure [between 1980 and 1987] from certain members (the auditing group) of the Council". Third, "those in the profession may seek to maintain their economic advantage by keeping the supply of qualified accountants and auditors low". Fourth, members of the auditing sub-system rejected "the MSc because university qualified accountants had to be paid more than ACCA trainees who spend years being paid as unqualified staff". The MSc challenged (according to Margaret Mendes) the "belief and value system of the ICAJ/ACCA committed groups". [40]

However, Mendes highlighted a few practical problems:

> [There were] practical difficulties involved in relating a university postgraduate programme to the ACCA structure. From the ACCA side the change-over from the old examination structure already presented problems in evaluating components of courses now spread over three different papers. . . . The value of the university educational process could not be evaluated, and the differences which were strengths such as the research papers of the postgraduates were ignored. Exemptions became the major issue, which was not resolved.[41]

On the surface, the critique of the MSc's course content seemed to make little sense when it is considered that the MSc programme was a fruit of the partnership between the ACCA and the ICAJ on the one hand and the UWI on the other. The ACCA had, in fact, changed its strategy. The impasse also seemed to be counterproductive as far as increasing the number of Jamaican accountants was concerned and proved a constraint on the indigenization of accountancy following the 1980s.

Indeed, after 1982 the number of graduates at both the MSc and ACCA/ICAJ levels declined. Between 1976 and 1981 the MSc produced an annual average of eleven graduates. This figure declined sharply between 1982 and 1986 to seven, a period in which, as Mendes noted, the MSc came under increasing pressure. Graduates of the ICAJ/ACCA examinations averaged thirteen per annum between 1975 and 1981 and fell to ten per annum between 1982 and 1986.[42] The former relationship between the UWI and the ICAJ, which had favoured localized training and examinations for Jamaican student accountants, was fundamentally altered. This conflict reflected the overall concern about the virtues of "professional" and "academic" education. The consolidation of the MSc Accounting course that graduated its first class in 1976 had kept alive the project for localization.

A study by Mendes in 1983–84, while not focused on indigenization, observed several shortcomings in the training of accountants both by the UWI MSc and the ICAJ/ACCA joint examinations. Among the weaknesses of the ICAJ/ACCA joint examinations was the absence of indigenous content in the curriculum, which was determined by metropolitan (particularly in Britain and the United States) experience and lacked relevance to the Caribbean student. She observed the "negative effects of study package learning, an unstructured learning environment and the non-relevant content of the ACCA curricula".[43]

The UWI MSc programme did not escape Mendes's criticism. First, since professional theory and practice are integrally related, the MSc's main failing was the omission of practical experience during (rather than after) the course. Second, Mendes considered it a challenge for the MSc to be both a professional programme and an academic postgraduate programme at the same time.[44]

The suspension of the MSc course as a direct route to chartered accountancy crippled the indigenous accountancy movement in Jamaica. The hope for indigenization shifted to the wider Caribbean with the foundation of the Institute of Chartered Accountants of the Caribbean (ICAC) in 1989, which coincided with the suspension of the MSc qualification as a direct entry to the ICAJ. There was an understanding that ICAC would pursue Caribbeanization of accountancy by the establishment of a Caribbean qualifying examination.

As we will see, up to the end of the twentieth century, ICAC failed to conduct its first Caribbean examination.

Table 4.1. Comparison of Passes, 1982–1987

Level	Academic Period					
	1987	1986	1985	1984	1983	1982
1	51	44	33	47	43	42
2	31	33	36	17	14	6
3	18	14	18	9	4	5
All levels	100	91	87	73	61	53

Source: Annual Report 1986–87, 13.

Table 4.2. 1986 Results

Level	June			December			Total		
	Entered	Passed	%	Entered	Passed	%	Entered	Passed	%
1	218	20	9.2	227	24	10.6	445	44	9.9
2	274	12	4.4	289	21	7.3	563	33	5.9
3	40	6	15.0	50	8	16.0	90	14	15.6
All levels	532	38	7.1	566	53	9.4	1,098	101	9.2

Source: Annual Report 1986–87, 13.

It was not until 1991 that the ICAJ "lifted the suspension of admission of MSc Accounting graduates to the ICAJ, subject to periodical reviews of the programme".[45] The impasse was partly resolved by the growing acceptance that the ACCA (professional) and MSc (with its academic and research orientation) could not be identical. The UWI was expected, however, to ensure that its standards were in compliance with IFAC criteria.[46] The impasse was not fully resolved (at least immediately) since despite "lifting of the ban by the ICAJ some transnational audit firms still required holders of the MSc to pass the ACCA professional examinations before being recognized as Chartered Accountants within these firms".[47]

As the following chapter will show, the national accounting institutes in Jamaica and the Caribbean agreed to establish the Institute of Chartered Accountants of the Caribbean in 1989. Insofar as the Caribbean body had plans to organize a Caribbean examination, the story of ICAC is a continuation of the present chapter. Equally important was the hope that the ICAC would contribute to a resurgent movement for Caribbean integration.

Chapter 5

The Caribbean Connection: The Institute of Chartered Accountants of the Caribbean

Disagreements between the UWI MSc programme and the ICAJ between 1976 and 1991 did not end the vision of localization. For example, Carroll Thorburn held out the hope that the establishment of an accounting school in Guyana would lead to the localization of the professional curriculum and examinations.[1] Furthermore, the establishment of the Institute of Chartered Accountants of the Caribbean (ICAC) in 1989, which coincided with the suspension of the MSc as an entry route into the ICAJ, was, rather ironically, intended to further the process of Caribbeanization, with the cooperation of UWI.

Inevitably, Caribbeanization, as envisaged by the ICAC, became tied to the larger vision of functional Caribbean cooperation, including the establishment of the Caribbean Single Market and Economy (CSME). Allied to the formation of a Caribbean body of accountants was the position of IFAC: that the "input to the world body should be through regional organizations composed of countries which, geographically, are in close proximity to each other".[2]

The dissolution of the West Indies Federation in 1962 had simultaneously ended the movement for Caribbean political integration and focused attention on functional cooperation among member states of the former federation. With the concept of functional cooperation superseding political integration, the Caribbean Free Trade Area (CARIFTA) was established in 1965, the Caribbean Regional Secretariat (1968), the Caribbean Development Bank (1969) and the Caribbean Community (CARICOM) through the Treaty of Chaguaramas and the Caribbean Examinations' Council (CXC) in 1973. The first Treaty of Chaguaramas was signed on 4 July 1973, by Barbados, Guyana, Jamaica and Trinidad and Tobago. Apart from these institutional arrangements there were sometimes mutual exchanges on the stock markets of Barbados, Jamaica, Trinidad and Tobago, and St Lucia, though the ultimate dream of a unified Caribbean stock market never materialized. The movement of capital within the Caribbean was probably based more on pragmatic assessments of profitability than on a commitment to Caribbean cooperation.

With the Grand Anse Declaration in 1989, the anglophone Caribbean governments made an ambitious commitment to move by stages, from the CARICOM status quo towards the establishment of a Caribbean Single Market and Economy (CSME). The immediate and long-term relevance of the CSME to the Caribbean accounting profession rested in its advocacy of the free movement of skills and services within the Caribbean. The revised Treaty of Chaguaramas in 2002 removed existing trade barriers and allowed, in theory, for the free movement of skilled professionals within the Caribbean, including, of course, accountants.

The Caribbean political directorate's support of the CSME did not arise solely from a sentimental attachment to Caribbean integration. The support came partly out of a somewhat hostile international economic environment, which threatened to marginalize the Caribbean. The Caribbean political directorate fully recognized that the new international dispensation of trade liberalization and globalization of production promised (or threatened) by the establishment of the WTO and the General Agreement on Trade in Services (GATS) ensured that the Caribbean "must of necessity, work together". Jamaican prime minister P.J. Patterson emphasized the importance of the free movement of skills to functional cooperation.[3]

The experience of the CXC was to prove that the challenges of harmonization of interests in the Caribbean could only be met successfully with high levels of determination, commitment and significant financial inputs from Caribbean governments. Dr Dennis Irvine, the second chairman of the Caribbean Examinations' Council (CXC) and vice-chancellor of the University of Guyana, in summarizing the challenges faced by the CXC in promoting a unified Caribbean examination, gave a preview of the structural challenges that applied to most efforts at Caribbean cooperation:

> One of the major problems facing CXC is trying to encourage national development simultaneous with Caribbean integration. Due to the different stages of development and the varying ideologies of Caribbean territories it has been difficult to formulate plans, which do not conflict with national development. The CXC is attempting, eventually, to satisfy the region's educational assessment and evaluation needs, by trying to find an examination that will cater to the region generally while preserving the national characteristic of territories that subscribe to it.[4]

Caribbean Regional Accountancy

The policy of Caribbean governments that advocated functional cooperation was not the only factor that encouraged greater cooperation among Caribbean accounting bodies, which led to the launch of a regional body of accountants in 1989. Caribbean accountants, identifying common interests, had been cooperating among themselves long before the establishment in 1989 of the Institute of Chartered Accountants of the Caribbean and the Grand Anse Declaration of that year.

The idea of a unified body of Caribbean accountants had been discussed as early as July 1967 with an exploratory meeting between Barbados, Guyana, Jamaica and Trinidad and Tobago, and a second meeting in Barbados in December 1969. Predictably, the proposal for closer cooperation was linked to the economic development of the Commonwealth Caribbean. Second, the training of accountants had, of necessity, to be focused on the Caribbean area since the passage of the Commonwealth Immigration Act of 1966 had reduced the opportunity for many potential Caribbean students to study in the United Kingdom. Third, economies of scale recommended a larger pool of members. With only 132 members in 1968, ICAJ membership fees were high.

Progress towards a Caribbean apex body was slow. President J.F. Lord, of the ICAJ, confessed in his report to the Council in 1971 that no progress had been made with respect to establishing an "Apex" Caribbean body, partly because of major lags in Caribbean legislation. However, by 1974 Jamaica (ICAJ, 1965), Trinidad and Tobago (Institute of Chartered Accountants of Trinidad and Tobago, 1970), Barbados (Institute of Chartered Accountants of Barbados, 1974) and Guyana (Institute of Chartered Accountants of Guyana, 1974) had established their own institutes of chartered accountants. By 1974, therefore, the basis existed for cooperation between functioning accountancy organizations in the Caribbean. In 1972 Trinidad and Tobago offered reciprocity of membership between the ICAJ and ICATT.

High on the agenda of accounting institutes in the Caribbean was the revision of company law, which from the wider Caribbean perspective, was in an anarchic state. It is true that original company law legislation was based on UK laws, but none of the Caribbean nations had kept up to date with the British law, much less set up their own legislative procedures. The 1965 Jamaican Company Law was based on the 1948 British law. The Guyanese Companies Act was based on the 1908 British Company Law, with modifications in 1961 based on the 1948 UK legislation. The updated United Kingdom Company Acts of 1967 and 1976 (and 1985) had been for the most part ignored.[5] The efforts of the ICAJ and other Caribbean institutes to revise the company law were rewarded with a proposal for a new company law in 1987, coinciding with the regimes of Aulous Madden (1985–87) and Donald Reynolds (1987–89). However, intensive discussions continued with respect to amending the company law in the 1990s, culminating in the 2004 Jamaican Company Law. Even with the passage of the 2004 law, modifications continued to be recommended.

Company law reform was considered necessary because of the erratic way in which Caribbean territories had adopted bits and pieces of British legislation. A working party, which focused on the harmonization of Caribbean company law between 1975 and 1979, submitted a draft bill of approximately four hundred clauses to governments of the CARICOM member states in July 1979. Only Barbados, with its Companies Act of 1982, implemented, substantially, the major recommendations for company law reform in the working party's report. In 1986, the ICAJ (with the assistance of $22,000 from the PSOJ) researched the reform of company law in order to bring it in line "with similar laws in the Caribbean and in other countries".[6] Nevertheless, company law remained on the agenda of the ICAJ and other Caribbean institutes for a very long time. The question of insolvency was also placed on the Caribbean agenda, bearing in mind the need for harmonization of legislation in the CARICOM area.

Complementing the growing sentiment for functional cooperation in the Caribbean was the interest of the ACCA, which, it has been argued, desired to maintain a strong profile in the Caribbean accountancy market. In their 1976 visit to the Caribbean, Harry Hill, president of the Association of Certified Accountants, and Frank Osbourne, secretary of overseas relations of the ACCA, encouraged the foundation of a regional body of Caribbean accountants. Some of the proposed meetings were cancelled owing to lack of support by some Caribbean institutes, in spite of a grant from the Commonwealth Foundation to assist with the "start-up expenses".[7] The Eastern Caribbean islands, most of which were still British colonies at this time, proved particularly unenthusiastic. Eventually, institutes were established in St Kitts–Nevis, St Lucia, and Antigua and Barbuda, which merged in 2006 as the Institute of Chartered Accountants of the Eastern Caribbean. When the apex body was founded in 1989, the ACCA proved very supportive, and offered financial assistance to the ICAC between 1988 and 1994 to facilitate its operations.[8]

In the meantime, starting from 1976, the ICAJ established and maintained more formal contact with other Caribbean accounting institutions. The Caribbean Conference of Accountants, which took place between 21 and 22 April 1978 in Jamaica, is usually dubbed the "first" meeting of Caribbean accountants. In fact, as we have noted, that meeting followed earlier meetings in 1967 and 1969. The 1978 conference was, however, broader in scope, wider in representation, and reflected the growing momentum for a Caribbean apex body. This was a well-attended conference whose theme was "The Profession in the Third World", a theme directly addressed by UWI's vice-chancellor A.Z. Preston, who was also at the time chairman of the Public Accountancy Board. The conference included participants from Barbados, Guyana, Trinidad and Tobago, the Bahamas, Jamaica, the Cayman Islands, the Netherlands Antilles, England, Canada and the United States of America. At this meeting, the

Institute's president, Jasper Burnett, stressed the importance of Caribbean regional cooperation.

The ICAJ continued to play an important role in the establishment of a Caribbean-wide organization of chartered accountants by hosting annual meetings of Caribbean institutes following the 1978 conference. In 1983, the Caribbean Conference of Accountants meeting in Kingston unanimously agreed to establish a regional body of accountants. Follow-up meetings in Trinidad and Tobago and Barbados smoothed the road to the formation of a Caribbean-wide institute.

The decision to provide a "professional networking forum" for accountants in the English-speaking Caribbean on 24 May 1987 marked the culmination and formalization of relations that had been evolving since 1967. The resolution at the conference hosted by Trinidad and Tobago to establish a regional body of accountants to be dubbed the Institute of Chartered Accountants of the Caribbean (ICAC) was followed by the signing of a Memorandum and Articles of Association of ICAC in Jamaica on 28 October 1988. Present were the presidents of the institutes of the Bahamas, Barbados, Guyana, Jamaica, St Lucia, and Trinidad and Tobago. Representing the ACCA was the Deputy Secretary of the ACCA, who conferred the blessing of the ACCA by presenting a gift of the first seal of ICAC. The establishment of the ICAC was received with much international goodwill and solid Caribbean rhetorical support.

Jamaica's leadership in the ICAC's birth also took the form of providing office space for the ICAC at the Ruthven Road headquarters. Aulous Madden, immediate past president of the ICAJ, was a central figure in the establishment of the ICAC. He chaired the steering committee that organized the ICAC, prepared a draft memorandum of objectives and by-laws for the Caribbean body and served as the first president of the ICAC. Aulous Madden served in that capacity for a record seven years. The long-term objective, according to Madden, was to ensure the consolidation of the ICAC, since the view of the IFAC was that regional bodies often had a brief life.[9]

5.1 President Donald Reynolds, 1987–89. The launch of the ICAC in 1989 took place during his presidency.

Since the ICAC sought to be representative of the various Caribbean institutes, its board of directors was drawn, logically, from the various supporting institutes. Members of the Jamaican institute served in various capacities, including as vice-president, treasurer and chair of publicity matters. Since Aulous Madden, there has been only one Jamaican president of the ICAC – Garth Kiddoe, in 2006–7.

In May 1989, the ICAC was inaugurated with due ceremony at the Jamaica Conference Centre, attended by over three hundred chartered accountants and businesspersons from seven Caribbean countries. The ICAC, having received the approval of CARICOM Heads of Government, received observer status within CARICOM in 1988–89, and remained open to membership from the wider Caribbean, including the Cayman Islands and the Dominican Republic, both of which had evinced interest. The ICAC also had international affiliate members. By 2015 these were the ACCA, AICPA, CPA (Canada) and the ICAEW (which withdrew its membership in 2016–17 after twenty-eight years). Caribbean integration and functional cooperation were, however, the central themes in the creation of the ICAC. Jamaica's deputy prime minister P.J. Patterson – a committed Caribbean integrationist – saw the ICAC as "enhancing the process of Caribbean cooperation".[10] The keynote address by Trinidad and Tobago's minister of finance Selby Wilson went further by referring to the commitment of the Government of Trinidad and Tobago to Caribbean unity. Of even greater interest was his projection of the idea of an "indigenous" Caribbean Institute of Accountants:

> At present none of our national institutes of chartered accountants have a unique identity principally because our membership body has been trained and qualified under different requirements. Some are trained in the United States, Canada, England and others hold MSc degrees from the UWI. . . . In the Caribbean, for many years now, we have trained our doctors, lawyers and engineers, all of whom would be recognised as competent professionals in any international forum. Why then, can't we train our own accountants?[11]

Jamaican and ICAC president Aulous Madden emphasized the functional value of closer cooperation in the accounting field. The "common heritage" of the region, comparable problems of devaluation and inflation, and basic similarity in Caribbean accounting systems provided the energy for the creation of a Caribbean body of accountants. ICAC would search for a common agreement on harmonization of company law, which would add a Caribbean flavour to the law and facilitate the setting up of a Caribbean Stock Exchange.[12] Probably also bearing in mind that the Jamaican Institute had a membership of 456, Trinidad and Tobago 413, the Bahamas 180, Barbados 148, Guyana 45, St Lucia 38 and Belize 26 members,[13] Madden suggested that regional cooperation in accountancy had the potential to benefit the entire region through the combination of resources. "The coming into being of the ICAC, with three times the present number of Jamaican accounting students, will make such a training venture more economical." Speaking specifically of the relationship between the establishment of ICAC and the future of accountancy in the Caribbean, Madden declared, obviously with the CSME in mind, "In the long run, the ICAC will allow greater mobility of Caribbean accountants. Shortages in individual countries can then be met with surplus accountants in other countries. The pooling and sharing of information and other accounting matters will also be a great benefit to the entire region."[14]

5.2 President Aulous Madden, 1985–87. He was chairman of the steering committee that established the Institute of Chartered Accountants of the Caribbean in 1989. He was the first president of the ICAC and served in that capacity for seven years.

Funding for the activities of ICAC came primarily from subscriptions of member bodies, which paid in proportion to the size of their membership. A steering committee was appointed to meet twice per year to discuss issues of mutual interest. The ICAC, with its objectives of indigenizing accountancy examinations and harmonizing accounting and auditing standards in the Caribbean, has grown in membership, including affiliate and associate membership, over the years. It is true, however, that the UK-based ICAEW withdrew in 2016–17 and the Bahamas Institute ceased to attend meetings because of "miscommunication and misunderstanding" according to the ICAJ. The temporary withdrawal of the Bahamas, until 2006, was really more than miscommunication and misunderstanding,[15] but tensions did occasionally arise among Caribbean partners.

5.3 Caribbean Conference of Accountants, 2011

The twenty-nine-member Suriname Institute of Chartered Accountants became an associate member of ICAC in 2011 and a formal member in 2017.[16] The Turks and Caicos Islands Society of Professional Accountants (TCISPA) received associate membership in 2016–17. In 2008, there were discussions of membership of the British Virgin Islands Association of Professional Accountants (BVIAPA) and the Cayman Islands' Society of Professional Accountants. Although the territorial membership of ICAC has not extended much beyond the original seven members, membership in each territory has grown significantly. As of 31 December 2014, the Institute of the Bahamas had 493 members, Barbados 837, Belize 51, Eastern Caribbean 200, Guyana 94, Jamaica 1,131, and Trinidad and Tobago 1,239.

Freedom of Movement

The establishment of the ICAC and the movement towards functional cooperation in the Caribbean merged. Indeed, the inauguration of ICAC (May 1989) almost coincided with the Grand Anse Declaration (July 1989) that envisioned the Caribbean Single Market and Economy (CSME). It was understood, given the traditional balkanization of the Caribbean, that the ambitious CSME project could only be achieved through incremental stages and realistic deadlines. The existing trade barriers within the Caribbean territories were removed by the Revised Treaty of Chaguaramas in 2002. The CSME would now include services, capital, technology and the free movement of skilled professionals. The ICAJ appeared to accept free movement of professionals not only for the purposes of Caribbean integration, but also because Jamaica's output of accountants was then such that the Jamaican market seemed on the verge of saturation. There was "now an over-supply of qualified professional Accountants. This has resulted in our members finding it extremely difficult to find jobs commensurate with their qualifications."[17]

The Revised Treaty of Chaguaramas (2002) promoted freedom of movement of professionals and explicitly advocated the harmonizing of the law and legal systems of member states in the interest of a functioning CSME. The subject areas identified in the treaty for harmonized legislation had a distinct bearing on economic growth and integration within the common market. The liberalization of trade in services, which was expected to follow the implementation of the CSME, drove the regional programme. Institute of Chartered Accountants of the Caribbean was expected, in part at least, to be the channel through which "common or harmonised qualifications would allow for free movement of professionals to facilitate the processing of licenses for practitioners to work in CSME territories other than their own".[18] The ICAC's objective to establish the same (or at least comparable) entry level qualifications among all territories within the region was to find significant stumbling blocks.

Meeting the challenge of common qualifications to ensure free movement of professionals was fraught with challenges. For example, in 1997, all the Caribbean institutes recognized membership in the following bodies as a sufficient condition for membership – ICAEW, ACCA, CICA and AICPA. All the institutes, except the ICAJ, recognized the CGA-Canada. The reluctance to include the CGA was the result of Jamaica's insistence on IFAC's auditing practice regulations. However, closer relations with the CGA accompanied the drive for harmonization of accountancy qualifications across the various Caribbean institutes. Trinidad and Tobago and St Kitts also included CIMA (Canada). St Lucia and Trinidad and Tobago accepted AIA, which the ICAJ had consistently refused to admit to membership, although the AIA, founded in the United Kingdom in 1928, was recognized by the UK government under the Companies Act of 2006.The ICAS and the ICAI were recognized by all of the institutes except BICA. Only Jamaica recognized the UWI Mona MSc (Accounting). Up to 1997 "mutual recognition was not provided for by any of the institutes, except for Trinidad & Tobago, which provided reciprocal membership".[19]

5.4 Donald Reynolds, Raphael Gordon, Alfred Rattray at ICAC conference in 1999 in Barbados

The limitations of cooperation were realistically recognized. It was true that there were some territories within the Caribbean that needed qualified accountants. On the other hand, although CARICOM had agreed, in principle, to the free movement of professionals, some territories were likely to impose restrictions on movement, whether resulting from individualism and insularity, or from a jealous defence of sovereignty and protection of the labour market from the entry of nationals from other Caribbean territories. The ICAJ seemed willing and able to entertain an inflow of accountants from other parts of the Caribbean, on two conditions: first, that the ICAJ and PAB work closely together to ensure that only the highest quality services were delivered in the Jamaican market in the issuing of practising certificates.[20] Second, establishment of business in Jamaica, the largest part of the English-speaking Caribbean market, required either Jamaican citizenship or Jamaican residential status.[21] Work permits, the anticipated Skills Act and the Public Accountancy Act would, together, ensure Jamaica's interests.

Relations within the Caribbean and within ICAC were marked, as always, by both dissent and consensus. The occasional tensions between Caribbean states, including at immigration counters, always posed challenges to genuinely free movement of professionals within the Caribbean. In 1998, Prime Minister Mitchell of Grenada admitted that "Free movement of skills in the region, which we all agreed to implement, is not working as envisaged."[22]

Caribbean functional cooperation and indigenization of accountancy became interlinked, at least in theory. The story of Caribbean efforts at harmonization appears to confirm Ian Boxill's conclusion that there is no consistency in concepts of functional Caribbean cooperation.[23] In the midst of functional cooperation, the underlying insularity prevails. As the economic crisis of the 1990s permeated the Caribbean – no doubt partly caused by globalization – the more prosperous Caribbean centres such as Trinidad and Tobago and Barbados showed reservations about intra-Caribbean migration, notwithstanding membership of CARICOM. At a meeting of ICAJ on 23 November 2008, a member of the Council noted the reservations of the prime minister of Barbados about the CSME, "as too many persons were moving into Barbados and putting a strain on its social services". The ICAJ meeting also noted that CARICOM nationals were being discriminated against in favour of non-CARICOM persons who had been attracted by Barbados's policy of lowering tax rates for overseas companies. [24] There are no available figures yet to indicate if Jamaican accountants moved south to practise in other CARICOM territories. What is more certain is that Jamaicans moved north to the United States and to Canada rather than to the southern Caribbean.

Caribbean Accountancy Examinations

Among the objectives of ICAC was the localization of Caribbean accountancy exams. In 1987, the steering committee met with the UWI to coordinate the structuring of a common examination for the region, in conjunction with assistance offered from the Chartered Association of Certified Accountants (ACCA/CACA).[25] The ICAC's plan for one qualifying Caribbean examination, which would replace the existing UK-based system, involved collaboration with the UWI.[26] An MOU was signed between ACCA, ICAC and the member territories of the ICAC to enable students to become members of both the relevant national institute and the ACCA. The costs of the examination would be borne by the ACCA.

The ICAJ collaborated with the other ICAC members to harmonize qualifications for entry into the profession. Professor Randolph Williams (UWI) was optimistic, in spite of limited financial resources and poor administrative arrangements, but a Caribbean examination, he believed, for the accounting profession "must contribute to a greater awareness of the Caribbean environment and institutions and a deeper understanding of the relationship between accounting and finance and the development of the Caribbean region".[27]

In 1994, there were discussions regarding the establishment of a School of Accountancy on the UWI Mona campus that would, it was planned, operate "like the Norman Manley Law School at UWI".[28]

The minimum requirement for entry into the ICAC examination was a master's degree in Accounting or Level II of ACCA or its equivalent. The minimum requirement of a master's degree was a reflection of the impasse between the UWI and ICAJ in 1987–88.[29] Significantly, in its plans for indigenization, ICAC included examinations in tax and tax management and company law, with a Caribbean focus. The agreement was that accountants from Canada, the United Kingdom or the United States would be required to sit exams in Caribbean tax and company law in order to become members of the local bodies. This apparent victory for the localizers was short-lived, because after several years and many promises, ICAC proved unable to mount a Caribbean examination.[30] The hope of the ICAC to launch examinations in 1991 and 1994 failed to materialize. Textbooks for Caribbean taxation and company law, advocated since at least 1973, were not ready. Sample questions and answers, which were to be approved by ACCA, were not for the most part prepared. This is not to underestimate the problem of mounting such courses, which would have to be updated on a yearly basis. The cost of creating, revising manuals, setting papers would have been formidable. Previous lecturers at UWI created their own texts on law and taxation (unpublished presumably). The UWI, apart from the MSc, has introduced an MA in taxation.[31]

There were also disagreements between the main interested partners. The ICAC and the UWI were at odds, leading the ICAC to adopt ACCA examinations. The UWI, on the other hand, was at odds with both the ICAC, the ACCA and, to a lesser extent, the ICAJ. Therefore, Caribbean accountants, sitting the ACCA, continued to prepare British taxation and law papers. After much discussion as to the feasibility of holding final qualifying ICAC examinations in collaboration with the UWI and the ACCA, the directors decided to enter into a joint examination scheme with the ACCA and member institutes, similar to that obtaining with Hong Kong, Singapore and other countries.

There was also some tension between the ICAC and the ICAJ. The ICAJ effectively blocked the effort of the ICAC to transfer its headquarters to Trinidad and Tobago to coincide with the appointment of a new executive director (ICAC now has its own headquarters in Kingston). The fact that

ICAJ seemed convinced that "clear objectives for the ICAC were urgently needed" was indication enough that there were some disagreements between ICAJ and ICAC. For example, while the ICAJ now recognizes the MSc in Accounting (UWI Mona) as an avenue for entry into the ICAJ, the ICAC did not recognize the UWI MSc except indirectly when the MSc graduate was accepted as a member of the ICAJ. The ICAJ, however, remains proud of the achievements of those MSc graduates who became members of the ICAJ.[32] The ICAJ's chairman of the Future of the Profession Committee Patricia Hayle was supportive of the UWI's MSc:

> What are the concerns concerning the MSc? . . . The concern of the other Institutes in the region was in relation to the justification being used by Jamaica for admitting persons who are holders of the MSc qualification to membership, while not recognising qualifications such as AIA and CGA for admission. She [Mrs Hayle] advised that the reason why the Institute is so confident in accepting persons with an MSc qualification was its involvement in the development of the academic programme for this qualification.[33]

The UWI's approach was summarized in 1997 in the following three ways:

- an annual review of its programmes in light of the most recent US and UK programmes
- the incorporation of "recent" changes in the curricula of the professional programmes in the United States and the United Kingdom
- the recognition of "changing needs of Jamaica and the region with respect to the role of Accounting in the economic development of the region".[34]

The hope, then, for free movement of accountants in the Caribbean is a function of the will of Caribbean states to adhere to the spirit of the Grand Anse Declaration and the Revised Treaty of Chaguaramas. At the same time, adherence to Chaguaramas is related to the precarious social and economic conditions existing in these small Caribbean states. For the time being, the economic interests of the territorial states override functional cooperation and merge with a jealous defence of political sovereignty. In turn, disagreements among territorial partners on what constituted common entry requirements and common membership of ICAC had inevitable implications for the

Caribbean Single Market charter, which required harmonization of certification to ensure the latter's portability. With the Caribbean Single Market charter, the member bodies of the ICAC are moving towards a regime for the free movement of chartered accountants between territories. Once an individual is a member in good standing of an ICAC member institute, that individual will be accepted on application with a reference letter for membership of any other member institute. Past-president of the ICAJ Archibald Campbell and other members seem to believe that a Caribbean apex body is still a viable proposition, although some members have become frustrated with the relationship between ICAC and the ICAJ.[35] As for an indigenous Caribbean examination, discussions that started in 1989 still continue. The fruits of these discussions have ripened rather slowly.

Chapter 6

Crises and Reform, 1995–2015

This chapter examines the ICAJ's adaption to changing national and international realities and priorities.

The ICAJ's policy of promoting the training of professional Jamaican accountants had proven largely successful by 1990. On the other hand, indigenization, in the sense of developing a curriculum to fit the Jamaican and Caribbean environment, had been less successful for reasons we have outlined in the previous two chapters. The rift with the UWI had, however, been more or less healed. By 1980, the ICAJ had successfully established its own headquarters and devised plans for the expansion of the facility and of the secretariat for the benefit of students and members. The Institute had established a working relationship with other Caribbean institutes through the ICAC; deepened its partnership with the ACCA and the IFAC; raised its public profile; and expanded its membership and the student body. The *Charter* magazine and a newsletter kept members up to date on local and international events and issues. There was a deeper understanding with the PSOJ and the general business community, and, in particular, between 1980 and 1989 ICAJ members served actively as chairmen of government boards in the context of "restructuring" of the Jamaican economy by government.

Proud of its achievements, the Institute celebrated its twenty-fifth anniversary in 1990 with the publication of *The Institute of Chartered Accountants: The First Twenty-Five Years, 1965–1990*, edited by Jasper Burnett.

6.1 Celebrating ICAJ presidents past and present in 1990

Routine matters continued to engage the attention of the ICAJ. However, national and international circumstances starting in the mid-1990s redirected the energies of the ICAJ towards reform. The modification of outlook in the 1990s occurred because the long-term commitment to international harmonization of accounting practices converged and overlapped with a major national financial crisis, which resulted in the restructuring of financial reporting in Jamaica. The period from 1990 to around 2015 was marked by an interlinked process of internationalization and internal reform.

This chapter will also examine the convergence of the four major factors that drove reform. The first was the rapid growth and development of information technology. The second was the establishment of the World Trade Organisation (WTO) in 1995 that replaced the General Agreement on Trade and Tariffs (GATT), which had regulated world trade since 1948. The third was the collapse of some of Jamaica's financial institutions between 1996 and 1997. The fourth was the collapse of major US financial institutions, which not only accelerated changes already underway in the standards of international financial reporting, but also initiated the Great Recession.

The first part of the chapter will discuss the four factors involved in the crisis, and the second examines the responses of the ICAJ to the crisis.

Technological Change

Jamaica was very much a part of the great leap forward in technological change. With globalization and changes in technology, businesses transformed their administrative structures, introduced websites and e-commerce, restructured factories, brought marketing to new heights and pressed for business ethics and corporate social responsibility. Risk, always a factor in business, in this era of rapid change developed the sub-discipline of risk management, which was introduced within business and accountancy itself. New demands on educational systems to provide the expertise required for the service economy paralleled the uncertainties of the business environment. Education was now "education for uncertainty", or at best, education as lifelong learning. The equivalent of "lifelong learning" in the accountancy profession was continuing professional education/development (CPE/CPD). Information technology, which became a basic instrument of education, had two contradictory effects: improving efficiency and abolishing or reducing some areas of employment.

Information technology was the handmaid of globalization. The Institute, though not primarily a business organization, had no immunity against the changes imposed by globalization. The Institute, consistent with growing business practice, reformed aspects of its administration, introduced its website and e-commerce, and installed a computer laboratory to facilitate website research and individual internet access by students and members.[1] The renaming of the Library Committee as the Library and Website Development Committee by 2012–13, and in 2015–16 the Information and Communications Technology Committee, was not a cosmetic change. Rather, it reflected the growing importance of technology in the education of the Institute's student clientele. Between 2000 and 2001 the secretariat was "significantly" enlarged to accommodate technological advances. The George S. Willie Resource Centre, a gift from a US accountant (with Jamaican roots), improved internet access provided for the purposes of research, publications in accounting, taxation and auditing. The Resource Centre was officially opened 30 November 2011.[2] Changes in ACCA syllabuses, which responded to market demand, also mirrored continuing changes in the techniques of accountancy itself.

With greater momentum in the 1990s, the Caribbean (including Jamaica) adjusted itself to internationally driven changes, marked by the challenges posed by the continuous introduction of new technology and quick obsolescence. In 2000, governor of the Central Bank of Trinidad and Tobago Winston Dookeran remarked on how the availability of the new technology had forced the profession to "change focus" from "routine aspects" of accountancy to professional advisory services:

> The power and capabilities of computer technology are growing dramatically and knowledge bases are becoming more affordable and widely available. Many of the routine aspects of an accountant's work can already be carried out more efficiently by computer. The availability of basic financial analysis, budgeting and cash flow forecasting in software packages, means that these skills are now within the reach of non-accountants. It is, therefore, predicted that accountants will evolve towards providing a more professional advisory service. . . . Accountants were becoming "Knowledge" workers, who primarily add value through interpretation, analysis and interpretation, analysis and presentation of information, [and] will become more valuable as the economy becomes more service-based.[3]

The WTO and GATS, 1995

Familiarization with the new technology was accompanied by the further challenge of the cross-border movement of accountants, as proposed by the WTO and its subsidiary, the GATS. The foundation of GATS was an aspect of the story of harmonization of accountancy practices and of the free international movement of accountants. Proposals for harmonization obviously emerged because of the considerable variations among nations in accounting practices, which made it difficult for professional organizations to ensure common standards. "Some countries require what others prohibit."[4] There was, also, the challenge of reconciling financial reporting based on local law with reporting by transnational companies, which had to "comply with the rules prevailing in their country of origin".[5]

The principle of harmonization was not new, but now received a more urgent emphasis. In its report, the Group of Eminent Persons, appointed by the United Nations in 1973 to study the impact of multinational corporations on development and international relations, drew attention to a serious lack of both financial and non-financial information in usable form on the activities of transnational corporations and the limited comparability of corporate reports. The UN Group considered that in order to remedy these deficiencies, an internationally comparable system of standardized accounting and reporting should be formulated and, to this end, it recommended that expert groups be convened under the auspices of the Commission of Transnational Corporations.[6]

The World Trade Organization (WTO), which succeeded the General Agreement on Trade and Tariffs (GATT) in 1995, intensified efforts towards harmonization of international accounting standards, and brought some of these ambitions to fruition at the end of the twentieth century. The WTO and the GATS accelerated efforts to harmonize private and public sector financial reporting.

The WTO was one of the fruits of neoliberalism (or the new liberalism). The drive towards neoliberalism began, essentially, with the Washington Consensus of 1981, which reasserted the principles of free trade, free movement of capital, deregulation and a diminished role for the nation state. State-owned businesses were, in this dispensation, to be privatized and placed in the hands of the private sector.

GATS, the professional equivalent of the free movement of capital, advocated the removal of all "unnecessary barriers to trade in accountancy services".[7] The WTO, as an intergovernmental organization, committed governments to uphold GATS regulations that included *Disciplines on Domestic Regulation in the Accountancy Sector (Disciplines)*. With respect to accountancy, the GATS defined trade in services "broadly to encompass accounting and audit services delivered across borders via electronic technologies, direct foreign investment in accounting and auditing firms, and the movement of professional workers across borders to practice as accountants and auditors".[8] Critics of GATS argue that the *Disciplines* could potentially "undermine domestic regulation and local autonomy".[9] But that was precisely what they were intended to do.

The IFAC, of which the ICAJ was a member, supported the GATS proposals insofar as they provided "worldwide guidance" for the profession; endorsed "reciprocal recognition of professional accountancy qualifications between nations"; recognized the increasingly international character of the accountancy profession; standardized the profession's approach to Mutual Recognition Agreements (MRA); and facilitated cross-border practice.[10] IFAC's only reservation was that the GATS *Disciplines* had not gone far enough to ensure a "free market in accounting services".[11]

The World Trade Organisation (WTO), the face of the new globalized order, received the support of IFAC and, of course, its members, including the ICAJ. Support for the adoption of International Accounting Standards (IAS) also came from multilateral agencies such as the Inter-American Development Bank (IDB), the World Bank, the IMF and the Organization of Economic Cooperation and Development (OECD) who offered institutional support (that is, funding) to advance the process of harmonization of international accounting standards.

Views coming out of the ICAJ showed a leaning towards the harmonization of accounting practices through the implementation of IAS. The process favoured transparency, greater business confidence in financial reporting, and a more business-friendly environment in Jamaica.[12] Yet, there were, understandably, a few reservations. ICAJ's president Raphael Gordon recognized that the GATS programme had encouraged an influx of foreign practitioners who placed the Jamaican profession under severe pressure. "The global market place," declared the president, "has created significant competition to our profession, and there is an inflow of overseas practitioners, who are seeking work to boost their revenue base. The professionals have secured a number of government engagements."[13] And so emerged the ghost of times past when the profession was dominated by non-Jamaicans. Foreign Direct Investment (which encouraged foreign firms to operate in Jamaica) and the international mobility of accountants was a tide against which the ICAJ could not easily swim.

In any case, the financial crisis in Jamaica in the late 1990s persuaded the ICAJ and the Ministry of Finance to make internationally based harmonization of financial reporting the norm.

The Jamaican Financial Crisis

The commitment of the Jamaican government to neoliberalism in 1989 included deregulation and the removal of foreign exchange controls. The new policy was, at first, greeted with enthusiasm by some businesses, which believed that neoliberalism would awaken a new entrepreneurial spirit in Jamaica. The most optimistic businessmen even assumed that the burden of the foreign exchange crunch – a feature of the island's economy since the late 1970s – would be lifted.

There was some uneasiness on the part of the president of the ICAJ, Everton McDonald. His view was that the ICAJ's by-laws were being breached by some businesses who interpreted deregulation as a signal for a greater "free for all". In this "free for all" the pressures on the local accounting profession would increase "as, so far, the regulations for acceptable conduct in a market environment such as anti-trust legislation have not been put in place".[14]

Uriel Salmon, in an interview with *Charter* magazine, cleared accountants of blame for the financial crisis. But there were a number of people in top positions in business, he argued, who were never trained "and they're now beginning to find out that family stock can't run business; you need education and experience".[15]

The view gradually emerged that Jamaica's adoption of a deregulation policy, even if necessary and inevitable, was premature. Deregulation, as it turned out, brought competition from imports, for which Jamaican entrepreneurs (accustomed to protection) were not always prepared. Nor did it lead automatically to availability of foreign exchange that had made life difficult for Jamaican businesses from the 1970s through the 1980s. Some businesses, even some successful ones, found it difficult to survive, though it is also true that some major companies globalized themselves, taking advantage of the new technology and launched themselves on a course of international competitiveness. The "free for all" no doubt helped to create the crisis, the major manifestation of which was that the years from 1990, even more than the 1970s and 1980s, were marked by the rapid depreciation of the Jamaican dollar and an inflationary spiral. A number of major Jamaican financial institutions (including Workers' Bank, Century National Bank, Crown Eagle and National Commercial Bank) collapsed in 1996–97. Some institutions were rescued by government; others died, without hope of resurrection.

Debates on the causes of the financial collapse, which have been interpreted in various ways, will not detain us. From the point of view of minister of finance Omar Davies, the collapse had resulted from poor business management. He hinted at an ethical problem when he urged accountants "working within corporations as well as independent auditors to adhere to strong ethical standards to ensure that financial statements conform to the highest standard".[16] Veteran accountant and foundation member of the Institute Philmore Ogle agreed with the minister on the question of ethics. "For too long the code of ethics has given the impression that members not in practice are not accountable for the ethical and reporting responsibilities of the companies which employ them."[17] Ogle's response underlined the long-standing concern about the ICAJ's lack of legislative and regulatory power to control the standards of non-members of the Institute. Over-speculation by the failed financial institutions and the high interest rate regime of government came in for their share of blame for the crisis.

Following the collapse of Jamaican financial institutions, the government, in 1997, embarked on the rescue of some financial institutions through the Financial Sector Adjustment Company Limited (FINSAC). The ICAJ itself looked to new strategies to avoid future crises.

International Crisis

As if the local crisis was not enough, at the start of the twenty-first century there emerged an international economic crisis leading the way to the "Great Recession" of 2008–9. US financial institutions such as Enron, World Com, Parmalat and other international companies collapsed. The Financial Crisis Inquiry of 2011 concluded that the recession was a result of failures in financial regulation; the dramatic breakdown in corporate governance; recklessness of financial firms in risk taking; and "a systematic breakdown in accountability and ethics at all levels".[18] The collapse of these overseas institutions accelerated the need for reform of the accountancy profession itself.

Response to Crisis

Increasing accounts of fraud in a number of businesses, bad or doubtful debts, and a worsening of the general economic climate convinced ICAJ president Raphael Gordon that serious consideration had to be given to internal controls of the accounting profession.[19] The crisis in Jamaica had not, of course, been created by the accounting fraternity, but the fraternity was deeply concerned in cases where its members had colluded with businesses in misrepresenting audited accounts in violation of ICAJ regulations. According to Gordon:

> It is public record that the audit of at least one of the failed banks was seriously deficient and that that institution fired its auditor to seek a more accommodating one before ending up in FINSAC'S arms. In my

roles as a member of a credit committee and as a financial consultant, I see audited financial statements that are so palpably misleading that I am embarrassed for my profession.[20]

The sitting president of the ICAJ, Patricia Hayle, declared that "rightly or wrongly our profession is viewed as having contributed to the economic malaise in which the country finds itself".[21] The point of view of the Minister of Finance Davies was that companies, in the face of competition, had resorted to "manipulation to enhance the level of earnings presented for public consumption".[22]

The ICAJ considered self-regulation essential. On the other hand, the minister of finance, while congratulating the ICAJ on its self-regulation policy, responded to corporate failures in Jamaica not only by establishing FINSAC, but also by increasing the regulatory capacity of the Bank of Jamaica (1997) and by introducing the Financial Services Commission (2001) as Jamaica's first "integrated regulator".[23] The new government controls would complement the profession's efforts at self-regulation. The ICAJ supported the government's efforts to rescue the failing financial institutions viewed as vital for the economic stability and development of the country. The Institute, clearly hoping that self-regulation would be the antidote to usurpation of function by the Bank of Jamaica, nursed grievances about the newly imposed regulations, which made the duties of auditors more "onerous" and had the potential to create jurisdictional conflicts. ICAJ president Eric Crawford noted that the new regulations also placed additional powers in the hands of public servants who were infamous for their "arbitrariness and arrogance".[24] A newsletter article "Can Auditors Be Jailed for Not Reporting?" identified one of the major reservations that some members of the accounting fraternity held with respect to the punitive clauses of the new government regulations: "This is, indeed, a first, as it imposes criminal liability on the auditor, not necessarily for failing to observe certain things, but for not reporting them or not carrying out the Supervisor's directive. This imposition of criminal liability is probably a first in the world. The Institute has strongly conveyed its opposition to the penal clauses. However, they were still retained in the amendments."[25]

The question of the protection of auditors from litigation continued to be discussed through 2007–8. The Institute was sufficiently concerned about the threat implied in the legislation to propose the engagement of a researcher to look into "the proposed legislative options in other jurisdictions to protect auditors from litigation. The committee noted that other countries were also researching this issue."[26] Later, with the strong urging of the ACCA, indemnity insurance for auditors was introduced. The idea of indemnity insurance for accountants and auditors had been broached by the Council between 1986 and 1988. The principle was accepted in 1988 but was not made mandatory.

Outside the new regulatory framework – which created anxiety at the Institute – there were significant areas of agreement between the minister of finance and the ICAJ. Both parties agreed that reform was necessary, that the road to reform was the adoption of international accounting principles and that reform was directly related to the encouragement of foreign direct investment.[27]

Members of the ICAJ argued that the crisis was partly systemic. The existing system did not allow ICAJ to enforce standards for *all* members of the profession, including non-ICAJ members. In an elaborate paper entitled "Legal and Administrative Framework for the Practice of Accountancy in Jamaica", the Institute recommended legal and jurisdictional solutions to safe-guard the profession's reputation and avoid the "violations such as those recently unearthed by FINSAC".[28] There was agreement on issues of enforcement, self-regulation and acceptance of IFAC's ethical, corporate governance and international financial reporting standards. It is in this context that ICAJ presidents Patricia Hayle (1999–2001) and Garth Kiddoe (2001–3) identified the vision of the ICAJ as inextricably linked with international (specifically IFAC) regulations.

Patricia Hayle, the first female president of the ICAJ, was uncompromising on the question of internationalization. "This is the dawn of a new era. The significance of 2000–2001 is not merely one of chronology. It is about rethinking the way we do business. . . . This is the era of globalization. Accountancy in Jamaica must adopt international standards and an international approach." The rather dramatic Hayle declared that the previous orientation of the Institute towards nationalism and indigenization had to be modified under the changing circumstances: "The milestones of the past 35 years notwithstanding, as the Institute stands poised to face the twenty-first century, it is with the recognition that the operational environment of the mid 1960s, defined largely by national imperatives, is today being re-defined by the changing paradigms of globalization."[29]

6.2 C. Patricia Hayle, 1999–2001. C. Patricia Hayle was the first female president of the ICAJ. Her term was responsible for several initiatives with respect to the increased powers of the ICAJ and the PAB in the regulation of the profession, the introduction of IFRS, as well as improved facilities for students.

Garth Kiddoe succeeded Patricia Hayle in the midst of the failures of Enron, WorldCom and other international companies. Kiddoe linked the international and national crises. The crises were catalysts for greater "self-policing" by the Institute, greater transparency, and restoration of eroding investment confidence in corporate governance and in accounting and auditing processes.[30]

The reform of the ICAJ, and of the profession as a whole up to 2016, included three major undertakings: first, promoting greater self-regulation; second, adopting IFAC's Code of Ethics and incorporating the Jamaican Bar Association to serve on the Institute's investigations committee; third, the introduction of general international accounting standards (IAS/IFRS) in 2002.

Code of Ethics

The formulation of a new international Code of Ethics came partly from the recognition that the accounting profession faced a crisis that was not only national and international but also moral and ethical. The new situation dictated the adoption in Jamaica in July 2000 of IFAC's Code of Ethics. There was no illusion by the parties involved that all abuses would cease, however. [31]

It is true that through its investigation and disciplinary committees, the Institute had responded, with some frequency, to alleged breaches of its by-laws, which allowed for reprimand, suspension, fines and even expulsion. Since the contemporary situation demanded more, the new IFAC Code was made mandatory for all the Institute's members. In 2006 ICAJ, in a comparison of IFAC's and ICAJ's Code of Ethics, found that "there were three sections of the ICAJ's Code that were not covered in IFAC's Code. These were (1) Tax Practice (2) Cross Border Activities and (3) Professional Competence and Responsibility regarding the use of non-Accountants". The Committee voted to retain these sections in the new code.[32] The IFAC Code of Ethics placed the public interest above that of the individual client or employer.[33] In 2001–2 the Institute proposed that its prospective members be required to take and pass a written test on the Code of Ethics before being admitted to membership.[34] Students were thereby exposed to the moral and ethical framework of the Code.

International Accounting Standards

The introduction of IAS was driven by global considerations and by local crisis and was designed to assure investor confidence, improve financial reporting compatibility, and facilitate the ability of local business to raise finance.[35] Given the convergence of international crisis and reform on the one hand, and the searchlight focused on the local profession following the internal crisis after 1997 on the other, the Institute could justify the adoption and adaptation of international formulas to national accounting and auditing standards to meet the needs of Jamaica.

The Accounting Standards Committee in 2000–2001 outlined very clearly the ICAJ's commitment to IAS, which were expected to become the mainstream reporting standards of the global economy:

> International Accounting Standards are expected to become the mainstream reporting standards of the global economy. As companies become more engaged in cross-border trading and the consequential increase in capital flows evolves, the need for an internationally recognized financial reporting system is heightened. The attractiveness of Jamaica's financial market system will, therefore, be supportable on a platform of high quality, globally accepted accounting principles. The proposal is therefore to migrate to full adoption of International Accounting Standards as of June 2002.[36]

The process of rethinking and retraining for the IAS/IFRS began with the local launch of pre-implementation seminars in 2001 by the Continuing Professional Education Committee. The date 1 July 2002 marked the beginning of Jamaica's reformed financial reporting procedures as the Institute fully adopted IAS – now International Financial Reporting Standards (IFRS) and International Standards on Auditing (ISA).

The implementation of, and compliance with, ISA and IFRS received a financial boost from a grant in March 2003 of US$665,000 from the Inter-American Development Bank (IDB). Under the agreement, the Institute provided matching contributions totalling US$350,000 in cash and kind over the life of the project. The project, initially proposed for a period of thirty-six months, consisted of four main components:

- Conduct of an independent assessment of accounting and auditing in Jamaica in accordance with the Reports on the Observance of Standards and Codes (ROSC) programme;
- Assistance in the implementation of IFRS;
- Building adequate mechanisms for the enforcement of IFRS and ISA;
- Establishing systems and processes that sustain the implementation of IFRS and ISA; and
- Using funds remaining at the end of the project to support the sustainability of the project.

The project, which received the first deposit of the IDB grant in April 2004, was launched on 11 June 2004 and was completed in 2008.[37]

The expectations of the IFRS were so continuous, numerous and complex that a witty Jamaican accountant remarked that the IFRS is "designed to make accounting impossible".[38] Both the government and the Institute rejected requests from influential private sector entities to delay the implementation of the IFRS. The Institute was itself so successful in the implementation of IFRS in Jamaica that during 2005 it received international recognition for the successful implementation of the programme. Impressed by the successful adoption of IFRS locally, the IFAC invited the Institute to share its implementation strategy, which would be included in IFAC's toolkit, "Establishing and Developing a Professional Accounting Body". The toolkit was to serve as a template for other countries implementing IFRS. The United Nations Conference on Trade and Development (UNCTAD) also selected Jamaica as one of five countries to be used in its case study on the effective implementation of IFRS.[39] Since Canada was scheduled to adopt IFRS in 2011 and the United States by 2013, we may conclude that Jamaica had been quick off the mark.[40]

Continuing Professional Education/Development

The changing business and financial reporting environment required members of the Institute to become "life-long learners". One of the requirements of the Institute to ensure professional standards was the CPE (Continuing Professional Education), which was renamed Continuing Professional Development in 2006–7. The concept of CPE/CPD, though now a requirement of IFAC, was not new to the Institute. A CPE programme had been initiated in the 1970s to enable members to keep up to date on financial and economic issues. At the time, President Jasper Burnett stated:

> Recognising that contemporary problems demand new strategies, the ICAJ provided opportunities for members to discuss questions of current economic and financial significance. The growing and urgent need for qualified accountants and the further development of the ICAJ as a strong and vibrant professional body were two imperatives that received our attention. The ICAJ directed its efforts to the necessity of attracting, training and *retraining* [italics added] suitable persons. This thrust will be maintained for the foreseeable future.[41]

Among the earliest subcommittees of the Institute was the Continuing Professional Education committee. Remarking on the work of that Committee, the president noted that "the Institute continues to place great emphasis on continuing education and has extended its activities to include the Caribbean region".[42] There was to be a minimum of twenty-one hours in any one year (and at least sixty-three hours in a three-year period) to be spent on appropriate structured courses.[43] An exception was made for retired registered members. The relevant by-law was amended in 2004–5 to reduce the standard minimum CPE requirement of retired but registered members.[44]

The CPE/CPD, for a long time a feature of the ICAJ's activity, was initially voluntary. The ICAJ stepped up its CPE programme by making it mandatory for its members from January 1998. Jamaican contributors to CPE, as of 1 January 2001, were "required to undertake at least thirty-five hours of continuing professional development".[45] Between 2005 and 2007, the ACCA phased in mandatory CPD (a more emphatic form of CPE) requirements for all members. The IFAC made it mandatory for accountants to upgrade their skills and knowledge, and to become life-long learners in response to the rapidly changing business environment and the changing contours of financial accounting. The IFAC's International Educational Standards (IES) Committee determined the minimum requirements for CPD.[46] The continuing education programme was conducted through seminars.

ICAJ and PAB

We noted earlier that the ICAJ considered the crisis of the 1990s to be the result of systemic weaknesses. In this respect, there was a grey area of uncertainty about the roles of the ICAJ and the PAB in the issuing of practising licences. The unclear division of labour between the ICAJ and the PAB had been evident from the 1970s. In April 1979, for example, both the PAB and the ICAJ asserted their separate rights to issue practising certificates. All accountants were not chartered accountants, and the Institute was not in a position to regulate the conduct of registered public accountants, who had been licensed by the PAB. The issue between the ICAJ and the PAB revolved around the reality that the ICAJ could discipline its members, but not necessarily practitioners licensed by the PAB. Cases brought to the ICAJ by the investigations and disciplinary committees were sometimes aborted because the ICAJ had no jurisdiction over such cases.

This particular issue, placed on the back burner since the late 1970s, came to the fore towards the end of the twentieth century and started off in the twenty-first century when the powers of the Institute were extended, and the PAB received greater disciplinary powers. The crises (national and international) forced a reassessment of the roles of the PAB and the ICAJ.

The responsibility for the regulation of entry into private practice rested with the PAB, which did not require evidence of practising experience from the Institute. In 1978, some 200 registered public accountants (RPAs) were practitioners who did not regard themselves as bound by the professional standards, which had to be observed by Institute members. The consequence was that with different standards being applied to ICAJ and non-ICAJ members, there was a concern that the profession in Jamaica could fall into disrepute.[47]

The view that the traditional relationship between the ICAJ and the PAB was in need of modification and that the relationship could not be sustained in light of the introduction of international standards led to a discussion about the merging of the two entities. The suggestion was rejected. It was understood, however, that the relationship between the ICAJ and the PAB would be determined in the future by the adoption of international accounting standards.[48] In any case, the ICAJ argued that it was in a better technical position to monitor the issuance of licences than the PAB. To strengthen its hand with the minister of finance, the Institute presented an elaborate lobbying document, "Legal and Administrative Framework for the Practice of Accountancy in Jamaica", in 2000. The document addressed the reality that not all accountants were "mandated" to observe all rules on ethics, the rules of CPE, of accounting and auditing standards as set by the Institute and determined by international standards.

Under the current regulations:

1. The ICAJ had no power to act in instances of breaches that were outside the ambit of the Institute.
2. The PAB had not developed mechanisms to monitor licenses issued to Registered Public Accountants.
3. The ICAJ requested that legislation be modified to assign the authority to license accounting to ICAJ practitioners.
4. In many instances, persons applying for and obtaining licenses from the PAB were not eligible for certification from ICAJ. The current status of legislation ensures that the practitioner's certificate from ICAJ can only be additional to, but not a substitution for, that issued by the PAB.
5. Of the 450 registered public accountants on record, at least one third fell outside the reach of the ICAJ. ICAJ, therefore, was unable to enforce compliance with rules to maintain the currency of technical education or CPE.

The outcome of all these discussions was that practising certificates required membership of the ICAJ and a practice certificate from the PAB. In addition, all RPAs were to be mandated to observe standards on ethics, accounting, auditing and the observation of the rules of CPE.[49]

The ICAJ, from as early as 2001, set its sights upon recognition by all accountants of CPE/CPD, the Code of Ethics and general international standards. The Public Accountancy Act was amended in June 2004 "to effectively monitor and ensure compliance of its members (RPAs) with a Code of Conduct as well as technical standards in keeping with those being met by members of the ICAJ". The amendments "strengthened the powers of the PAB to enable the Board to carry out its responsibilities as the entity issuing licences to applicants who qualify as public accountants. The PAB received more punitive powers."[50] The new arrangement increased the power of the ICAJ without making it absolute.

The government, through the minister of finance, designated the Institute "Sole official agents of the PAB". The designation, in practice, gave the ICAJ the responsibility to "establish and monitor experience requirements for all licencees, and evaluate the appropriateness of the experience of all applicants for licences". The PAB continued to register public accountants and issue licences in accordance with the provisions of the PAA, utilizing the newly determined criteria.[51] The criteria, as laid out, were not enough to avoid confusion in the minds of some as to the relative roles of the PAB and the ICAJ. The 2012–13 annual report noted the duplication of functions between both organizations.[52]

A further innovation was practice monitoring.

Practice Monitoring

The practice monitoring programme involved inspection or "quality assurance" visits to all firms – including sole practitioners. The enforcement of practice monitoring regulations was undertaken by the ICAJ, PAB and ICAC. A PSDP project (Private Sector Development Programme), funded jointly by the Government of Jamaica and the European Union, provided training for ICAJ practitioners and Registered Public Accountants (RPAs) in preparation for the proposed practice monitoring programme.[53] However, the PAB, ICAJ and ICAC (given the small Jamaican/Caribbean market) delegated their audit monitoring functions, through a four-year contract signed on 1 February 2011, to a senior practitioner reviewer (SPR) who was a specially trained officer of the ACCA (UK). The ACCA, chosen because of its vast international experience derived from monitoring thousands of accounts worldwide, assessed the extent of compliance with the International Auditing and Assurance Standards Board (IAASB) and the standards and Code of Ethics directly related to the conduct of audit work. The contract required the ACCA to provide detailed reports, findings and recommendations to the monitored firms and to ICAC, the ICAJ or PAB.[54] For ACCA members there was, for a time, an ACCA award to firms that demonstrated "best practice" in all aspects of their business during inspection by ACCA compliance officers.

The ICAJ and the Public Service (IPSAS)

The reform of accountancy practices extended to the public service. From the 1970s, ICAJ and ministers of government had queried the efficiency of accounting in the public sector. Minister of finance Dr Omar Davies insisted that accounting standards within the public sector should meet "stringent standards" and, like Douglas Vaz, the minister to whom the ICAJ had reported in 1981, emphasized the importance of cooperation between public and private sectors in the regulation of public sector accounting. Thus, the ICAJ and the minister of finance also shared common ground with respect to accountancy in the public service. Too often, Minister Davies concluded, "state officials, technical and political, tacitly, or even explicitly, assume that lower standards of accountability are acceptable within government".[55]

The Institute, as a member of IFAC and therefore committed to the international dimensions of the accountancy profession, urged the Government of Jamaica to introduce International Public Sector Accounting Standards (IPSAS) to bring public accounting into line with international standards. IPSAS, issued by the International Public Sector Accounting Standards Board (IPSASB), an independent organ of the IFAC, was favoured by some lending agencies. Although the Government of Jamaica, from the early 1980s, was fully aware of the need to reform public sector accounting, adoption of IPSAS was relatively slow. The Jamaican government accepted the principle of accrual accounting in 2002 "but quickly backtracked after the Ministry experienced technical and cultural difficulties".[56]

The ICAJ did not retreat. In September 2006, the Institute reasserted its obligation, as an IFAC member body, to "pressure" the government to make a commitment to IPSAS. In any case, IPSAS was "the standard required by the International Lending Agencies, Executive Agencies and all Budget Funded Bodies".[57] The ICAJ also offered its technical services to the Government of Jamaica in the implementation of IPSAS, as it related to for-profit government business enterprises (GBEs) and non-GBEs. Government business enterprises were subject to IFRS regulations. The government issued amendments to two critical pieces of legislation: The Financial Administration and Audit (FAA) Act and the Public Bodies Management and Accountability Act (PBMA) to adopt IPSAS by non-GBEs.[58]

We can assume that the formation of the Jamaican Association of Public Sector Auditors (JAPSA), which consisted of Internal Auditors who performed audit and inspection duties in central government and public sector entities, was one indication that the public sector was attempting to reform itself from within. JAPSA was scheduled to be launched 10 May 2000. The Institute's concern with the JAPSA, however, was that the Institute's standards were not sufficiently observed. The Institute turned down an invitation to attend and to mount a display at the launch. The Institute was sending a signal to JAPSA that the Institute's role had to be taken into consideration.[59] Happily, peace was made between the two bodies by the following year when mutual aims were discussed, and the JAPSA agreed to adopt CPE activities as a "platform for training". [60]

Professional Accountants in Business, 2016

The Professional Accountants in Business Committee was another initiative of IFAC.

Professional accountants in business are employees, consultants and self-employed owner-managers or advisers in commerce, industry, financial service, education and the public and not-for-profit sectors. PAIBs are essentially all other accountants who are not in a public accounting firm environment. The establishment of a PAIB Committee was undertaken based on the fact that over 70 per cent of our members are PAIBs, and there was no committee dedicated to meeting their specific needs. As such, the PAIB Committee was formed with the objective of increasing the awareness of the significant roles PAIBs play in nation building as well as to organize events that will create networking and knowledge sharing opportunities on topics relevant to PAIBs.[61]

Internationalism and the Broadening of Membership of the Institute

For some time, Jamaica continued to be one of the few, if not the only, Caribbean institute not to recognize the Canadian CGA, which required an undergraduate degree and CGA professional studies. The largest group of CGAs worked in the business sector, commerce, industry and services.[62] The CGA had a strong cross-Canada presence and was accepted in China, Hong Kong, Bermuda and in most of the Caribbean, especially in Barbados, where it had a high profile. The ICAJ agreed to recognize the CGA, partly because the harmonization of accounting qualifications across the Caribbean was essential for the free movement of accountants within the Caribbean Single Market and Economy. The ICAJ and CGA (Canada) signed an MOU in 2006, which opened the way for CGA members to enter the profession in Jamaica. The criteria applied by the ICAJ were IFAC's International Educational Standards (IES). The CGA was launched 2 October 2006, and CGA examinations were scheduled for March 2007. In any case, in January 2007 the ACCA announced a Mutual Recognition Agreement with CGA Canada in accordance with GATS regulations. In fact, the early twenty-first century saw membership of the ICAJ expanding to include the Canadian CGA, CMA (Certified Management Accountant) and CPA. The CMA in 2010–11 sought recognition similar to the earlier CGA.[63]

The internationalization of the ICAJ was also reflected in growing concerns about the environment. In response to global environmental trends, the Institute supported the establishment of clearer policy objectives governing standards in environmental accounting. Inevitably, matters of primary interest to metropolitan communities such as "money laundering"– often linked with the international drug trade – were to become issues of moment to national governments and accounting bodies. "Terrorist" financial activities and cross-border crime became another issue in the conduct and reporting of business transactions. [64] At a less structured level, relationships have been developed with ABASA (Association of Black Accountants of South Africa) and NABA (National Association of Black Accountants in the United States). The ICAJ, ABASA and NABA cooperate in their annual conferences.

Summary

The deeper integration of the international economy and the policy of harmonization of accounting procedures in the last two decades of the twentieth century succeeded in reducing divergences in accounting practices. In the late twentieth century, the replacement of GATT by the WTO and the foundation of GATS had a significant impact on financial reporting. The international crisis in the early twenty-first century brought to the fore the question of ethics and with it the adoption of the IFAC Code of Ethics, new systems of financial reporting (IFRS), and the harmonization of international accounting regulations. The harmonization of accounting and auditing procedures came closer to fruition with the crisis in international accounting at the end of the twentieth century. Events and processes between the 1980s and 1990s, including Jamaica's financial crisis, did much to encourage adoption of international standards. Meanwhile, new areas of accounting emerged: environmental and forensic accounting, new codes of ethics, and corporate governance. The solutions to the 1990s Jamaican financial crisis were found in the adoption of international regulations.

Chapter 7

Students and the World of ACCA Examinations, 1968–2015

This chapter is mostly concerned with the growth of the student body, the interaction between the Institute and its students, the performance of students in the Joint ACCA/ICAJ examinations (the ACCA, AAT and CAT), and the extent to which students played a role in advancing the interests of the student body.

The growth of the student body, which peaked at five thousand in 2007 was a factor – though not the only one – that motivated the ICAJ to expand its headquarters on a regular basis. By 1995, the expanding facilities included 2,400 square feet of additional office space coinciding with the thirtieth anniversary of the foundation of the Institute. The original single-storey residence was replaced by a two-storey establishment, which increased amenities for students, expanded library facilities, accommodated the student consortium and the ICAJ's Secretariat, and for a time, the Institute of Chartered Accountants of the Caribbean.[1] The headquarters also houses the George S. Willie Resource Centre, which was officially launched on 30 November 2011.

Recruitment of Students

In the 1960s, the production of some ten thousand pamphlets for distribution to secondary schools, and voluntary participation by Institute leadership at Career Day Expositions to encourage Cambridge or London GCE graduates (Ordinary and Advanced levels) to enter the accounting profession, indicated both the enthusiasm of the Institute to expand the accounting profession, and also to attract the best-qualified students.[2] From the 1990s the ICAJ had extended its recruitment activity to the growing number of rural schools, thanks to the expansion of the Jamaican educational system.[3] After 1975, another possibility for admission into the Institute's programme was for potential students with five 'O' level credits to pass the examinations of the Institute of Accounting Staff (IAS).[4] It will be noted, later, how patterns of recruitment changed over time.

In the early years, the Institute probably had to confront the reality that potential students of accountancy at the tertiary level preferred other areas of the social sciences such as economics, politics or business. Reservations about accountancy as an attractive and prestigious occupation compared to other branches of the social sciences seem to have continued in Latin America, according to a World Bank report in 2010.[5] In contrast, however, as early as 1987 accountancy and management studies became more important for career-seeking students in the Caribbean.[6]

A disincentive to enter the field of accounting was the high failure rate of ACCA candidates (as we noted in an earlier chapter), leading many students to abandon the enterprise altogether or perhaps not to start at all. Indeed, frustration with the ACCA examinations may have encouraged potential accountants to settle for the second tier. Another challenge was the time expended, and the financing needed, to complete all examinations from foundations through to professional examinations, in which the pass rate (national and international) was low. Those who completed in three years were regarded as exceptional. For example, a BSc in Accounting (three years) and a fifteen-month MSc at UWI plus two years of practice with a reputable firm added up to an investment of six and a half years of time and finances to achieve the distinction of becoming a chartered accountant. Preparation for the ACCA, while absorbing several years, did not bring a guarantee of completion in the context of a 35 per cent international pass rate.

The advantage that the ICAJ could most successfully press, at least in its early years, was the availability of employment in the field of accountancy, and the relatively good earnings of an efficient accountant in the private sector.

Growth of the Student Body.

Recruitment of students worked well. The Institute, as the clearinghouse for the ACCA, tended to accept over 90 per cent (with the exception of 1980–81) of the applicants. Figures for the available years show an increasing number of applications for the ICAJ/ACCA from 1980 to 1995.

Table 7.1. Admissions to ICAJ/ACCA, 1979–1994

Year	Applications	Admissions
1979/80	81	79
1980/81	143	81
1984/85	172	158
1985/86	188	171
1986/87	254	240
1987/88	294	268
1993/94	583	569
1994/95	816	813

Source: Annual Report 1979–95.

The student body grew significantly, in part because of the aggressive publicity campaigns of the ICAJ to promote the profession of accountancy among high school graduates. The student body grew from 242 in 1969 to 394 in 1971. By 1977, there were 1,188 students, whose numbers increased to 1,282 in the following year. As part of the publicity campaign, the ICAJ invited Prime Minister Hugh Shearer in 1971 to address the student body. There was a record turnout. The carrot extended to the prime minister was that many of the over 250 students were civil servants.

The sudden fall in student numbers to 774 in 1979 did not result from a declining interest in the profession, but from the Institute's decision to excise from its register students who "neither study, take examinations, pay dues, nor maintain contact with the Institute".[7] The number of registered students not paying their fees had, apparently, gone beyond the limits of paternalism. The number of active students rose to 861 in 1980 and returned to the one thousand mark (1,096) in 1988. From there on, student numbers continued to increase. By 1994, the student body exceeded 2,200, advanced to 3,831 in 2000 and peaked at 5,070 in 2007. The period 1980 to 1988 showed an increase of 29 per cent in the student body, compared with 123 per cent in the 1994 to 2007 period.

The increase in the student body attached to the Institute resulted both from stronger marketing by the Institute and from the significant increase in the number of accounting technicians. However, the growth of the student body was also related to the overall commitment of the Institute to improve the facilities available to students. The Institute has, collectively, been very committed to the welfare of its students, though it was generally understood that the "Institute had a larger role to play beyond examinations and student affairs".[8] The broader role was, in fact, the Institute's contribution to national development. Notwithstanding the protest of a member of the Council that student affairs were diverting the attention of the Council from attending to other urgent matters, the Council continued to improve the environment for students, including the provision of internet services.

Originally, student activities were firmly based in Kingston and St Andrew, but the Council began to provide facilities for students outside the Kingston Metropolitan Area, following aggressive lobbying by students.[9] Examination centres were established by June 1998 in Montego Bay, at Moneague and Knox Colleges, to accommodate candidates in western and central Jamaica. The Institute extended its opening hours to facilitate students' preparing for examinations, and introduced "rap" sessions outside Kingston and St Andrew in order to encourage candid contact between rural students and the ICAJ. At a "rap session" in Mandeville on 12 January 2008, students expressed concern that Knox Community College was the only tuition provider in Manchester for the professional examinations.[10]

ICAJ Student Society

The Institute's paternalistic relationship with its students ensured a student voice in matters affecting student welfare. The students were not always a passive element in their interaction with the Institute, which, in general, appears to have been encouraged, rather than frowned upon. The students' criticism of the Institute was sometimes frank and harsh.

The existence of an official student society, structurally linked to the Institute, did not preclude the formation of other student groups. For example, UTech students founded the Association of Accounting Students in 2007, and their peers at UWI established the Students' Association of Aspiring Accountants. Both associations appear to have been mostly concerned with developing closer relations with the ICAJ and guiding members on their journey towards becoming chartered accountants.[11]

However, it was the Students' Society that acted as the official voice of the students who were registered for the Joint ICAJ/ACCA Examinations. This Society had replaced an earlier student society that had been attached to the Jamaican branch of the ACCA prior to 1965.[12] However, a new student society was founded, thanks to Uriel Salmon and L.R. Reed, three years after the foundation of the ICAJ. The survival of the society was not left entirely to the transient and sometimes unpredictable nature of student leadership. Since the new society could be dissolved only by the Institute itself, continuity was, in theory, guaranteed by its structural link with the Institute, which provided the society with an annual subvention. Experience showed that the functional operation of the society depended partly on the ICAJ's intervention. Reports by Council, in 1985, and again in 2016–17 on the "reactivation" of the student society suggest that the society went through brief periods of relative dormancy. Students' meetings, except for an annual dinner and dance, could be explosive, and it was sometimes difficult to secure a quorum for annual general meetings.

The Institute regarded the relationship with the student society as "reciprocal". Students vacillated between mutuality and antagonism. Membership of the society, which was intended to further the professional advancement of students through cooperative study and social interaction, was a precondition for sitting the Institute's examinations.[13] While the society was described as open to all registered students of the Institute, it was not, strictly speaking, a voluntary association since the ICAJ *required* students to enrol as members of the Student Society.[14]

Students routinely channelled their recommendations, complaints and protests and, occasionally, their gratitude, to the ICAJ. In the late 1970s, before the establishment of the headquarters at Ruthven Road, students complained about the inability of the secretariat to respond to student requests for assistance and information.[15] There were protests against the quality of examination rooms, the attitudes of indifference of some members of the Institute, and absence of interaction between students and the Institute. In 1987, a correspondent to the editor of the *Daily Gleaner* went public. He attributed the "appalling" pass rate of ACCA students in the professional examination to the ICAJ's indifference and the poor quality of teaching. The correspondent called for the establishment of a school of accountancy.[16] The writer seemed less than impressed by the Student Accounting Training Consortium. However, from the point of view of the president of the Institute, the Consortium had succeeded in raising the pass rate in the professional examination from 0–10 per cent to 25 per cent.[17] A members' survey in 1999 reported that the majority of students considered the interaction between students and members to be either "non-existent or inadequate".[18] The survey, which coincided with a significant increase in students' fees, may have been badly timed.

Students sometimes questioned the way in which their fees were spent, but at the same time made explicit requests that the Council use its contacts with the accounting fraternity to assist them financially for training and study materials.[19] The regular depreciation of the Jamaican dollar made life more difficult for students. Affixed to a complaint about the poor standard of examination rooms was the underlying financial concern: "With one British pound sterling at $43 (at the time of writing this letter), the high cost of books, revision courses and classes, the opportunity cost of no-pay leave, and the mental stress of preparing for these exams, we do not need adverse exam room conditions adding to our problems. . . . We believe that the ICAJ should have taken a more keen [*sic*] interest in the affairs of its student body."[20]

Students almost always face challenges with financing their education. In this instance, the financial problems of students were aggravated not only by devaluation, and increase in fees, but by penalties imposed on them for non-payment of fees. The Students' Committee of the Institute reported in 1997 that the Institute "had come under a lot of fire from the student population, for measures seen as punitive, as the current penalty structure is 100 per cent for late payment of fees". It also reported that the Institute was "happy to report that the measures had proved effective, as the majority of fees due on

January 1, 1998 were collected within 30 days".[21] However, in October 2000, the ICAJ, faced with what it referred to as the hostility of the student body, recognized the importance of "minimizing" that hostility "to win them over as members by the time they qualify".[22] No doubt some of these frustrations arose from the financial situation of students, many of whom were struck off the list of registered students in response to their failure to pay their fees to the ICAJ/ACCA. The practice of removing students from the register, a practice extant in the late 1970s, may have fallen into abeyance after a few years, because there appears to have been no institutional memory of the excision of students from the register in the late 1970s, judging from the comment in the 1997 Annual Report that excision had taken place "for the first time" following a comprehensive exercise in April 1997. "Our data base now reflects all fee-paying students, rendering us better able to manage the resources to the benefit of the Student Society of the ICAJ."[23] In 2008, 1,001 students were removed from the scheme due to non-payment of ICAJ and/or ACA annual fees.

Another legitimate source of concern addressed by students was the training facilities. In 1980, they suggested that the ICAJ could be "more responsive in arranging regular examination work-shops and should endeavour to monitor more closely the standards of training".[24] They considered the teaching methodology of one community college inadequate and made the positive recommendation that the Institute monitor and accredit training institutions. The Institute's student committee consulted the ACCA Caribbean representative on the matter.

Students were also critical of the financial modus operandi of the Institute. They called attention, in 1996, to what seemed to them discriminatory funding. The Institute, they complained, provided scholarships to the UWI and none for ICAJ/ACCA students. There was also criticism of the length of time that the ACCA took to respond to their applications, resulting in uncertainty as to the exemptions to which they might be entitled.[25]

Just occasionally, the executive of the student body pointed to the lack of enthusiasm of the student body itself – an indifference that made it difficult for the student executive to lobby the Institute for improved training facilities.[26] There were occasions, such as in 1985, when the student body got its act together and persuaded the Council to subsidize ("highly", according to the

Council) "Workshops in Management Accounting, Quantitative Analysis and Costing" for the December 1985 diet.[27]

By way of encouragement, the ICAJ offered awards for excellent performances in the ACCA/ICAJ Joint Scheme Examinations. (High failure rates in some years do not detract from the excellent performances of many students over the years.) The practice of awarding prizes for excellent performances began as early as December 1969. Bruce Scott and Dion Staple at age twenty-one completed the ICAJ/ACCA Joint Scheme Examinations within three years.[28] Although male candidates have excelled, most of the awards now generally go to female graduates. In 1999 Carolyn Bell copped four major awards.[29] In 2003, seven of nine awards went to female candidates. Female students got six of the seven awards for outstanding performance in the December 2001 and June 2002 sittings of the ICAJ/ACCA Joint Scheme Examination.

7.1 Anecia Walters receives her Outstanding Performer award from Bruce Scott, sitting president of the ICAJ

Joint Examinations

The ACCA/ICAJ Joint Scheme Examinations – the route to chartered accountancy – constituted the apex of achievement for students. The joint ACCA/ICAJ examinations are strictly regulated and monitored by the London-based ACCA. Also linked with the ACCA/ICAJ alliance were the Institute of Accounting Staff (IAS) examinations (1975), the Association of Accounting Technicians (AAT) (1979) and the Certified Accounting Technician (CAT) (1997), which prepared second-tier professional accounting technicians. In addition, in 2011, the Foundations in Accountancy (FIA) was introduced. "The FIA consists of an introductory certificate in Financial and Management Accounting; Intermediate Certificate in Financial and Management Accounting; a Diploma in Accounting and Business, and the Certified Accounting Technician (CAT) qualification."[30] The FIA did not require a matriculation qualification. Completing the FIA, the AAT or the CAT were all potential roads leading towards the first-tier ACCA.

In all this, the Institute continued to rely on the mentorship of the ACCA. Up to 2016, the ICAJ resorted to requesting the ACCA for assistance in response to low passes in the Joint Scheme Examinations.

The table below shows that the Joint ICAJ/ACCA professional students increased by 35 per cent between 2000 and 2015; and that ACCA candidates, as a percentage of the total number of students registered, grew from 48 per cent in 2000 to 71 per cent in 2015. The core of the Institute's activity continues to be the ICAJ/ACCA professional examinations.

Table 7.2. Number of ACCA Students on Register at Three-Year Intervals, 2000–2015

Year	Number (ACCA)	Total Registration	Percentage
2000	1,842	3,831	48
2003	2,458	4,749	52
2006	2,865	4,902	58
2009	3,155	4,879	65
2012	2,754	4,214	65
2015	2,437	3,410	71

Source: Annual Reports 2000–2015.

The Student Accountancy Training Consortium

The student lobby kept the Institute on its toes. Aware that one of the students' frustrations was the low pass rate, the Institute encouraged the foundation of the Student Accounting Training Consortium in 1982, financed mainly by audit firms. The consortium enjoyed a considerable measure of success, at first. The consortium had a mixed, though generally favourable, response from students.

We have already noted D.C. Sale's belief that among the sources of student dissatisfaction was their poor examination performance. A comparison of results from 1982 to 1986 illustrates the limited success of students at the professional level, and the limited number of accounting graduates. It also shows an increase in the number of successful candidates in the post-1985 period.

Table 7.3. Passes in the ACCA, 1982–1986

Level	1982	1983	1984	1985	1986
1	42	43	47	33	44
2	6	14	17	36	33
3	5	4	9	18	14
Total	53	61	73	87	91

Source: Annual Report 1986–87, 13.

The Institute turned its attention to the improvement of student training facilities through the Student Accountancy Training Consortium in 1982. The challenge was not entry but exit. The slightly improved professional examination performance in 1985 and 1986 was most probably the result of the establishment of the Student Accountancy Training Consortium in 1982, workshops, quarterly lecture meetings and possibly the establishment of community colleges that prepared students for professional examinations. The establishment of the Student Accountancy Training Consortium was an initiative of students, led by Raphael Rowe with the cooperation of audit firms, which provided tutors and sponsored students. The ICAJ came into the picture through a staff member who was allowed time off to attend to the affairs of the Consortium. The ICAJ provided the Student Consortium with office accommodation and a subvention.

The consortium was established with the assistance of the training officers of Touche Ross, Pannell Kerr Forster, Mair Russell and Partners, and Coopers Lybrand, who pooled their resources to prepare students for the ACCA examinations. By October 1983, Capleton Jones, James Dewar, Lee Clark, Paul Goldson, Peat Marwick Mitchell and Price Waterhouse were added to the original four firms. "The presumption in those early days was that all audit firms would automatically become members and, in the case of the smaller firms, would be represented by Aulous Madden."[31] The consortium's financial resources were substantially improved with the participation of more audit firms. It received administrative support from the ACCA London and the ICAJ, which, at first, housed its secretariat. The hope that classrooms would be constructed at Ruthven Road never materialized, and the consortium purchased its own building at Parkington Plaza in Half Way Tree.

Students responded "overwhelmingly" to the organization of study schools by the consortium. They even succeeded in persuading the Council to subsidize special workshops in management accounting, quantitative analysis and costing for the December 1985 diet. Classes, which usually lasted for three months, were fully subscribed. The Institute encouraged the consortium and study school, but they remained separate organizations. Perhaps just as important was that the ACCA sponsored lecturers from the United Kingdom. The Institute observed that these lecturers were a "significant factor" in improved performances.[32]

Study schools, which began in 1986 and continued into the 1990s with sponsorship from the ACCA and the Institute, improved student performance. President Donald Reynolds reported in 1987–88 on the consortium's vital contribution to the increased pass rate in the joint examination scheme of the ICAJ and the ACCA.[33] Students saw a linear relationship between their success and the work of the consortium. For example, the most outstanding Level III student in 1994, Mrs Rose Campbell-Patrick, praised the consortium for the structured classes offered throughout the year. This graduate appears to have been particularly impressed by the lecturers invited from the United Kingdom to assist in examination preparation. The lectures "have proven to be extremely helpful in providing *first-hand knowledge* [italics added] of what is expected in order to pass the ACCA examinations."[34]

The figures available for the 1980s, nevertheless, indicate that the improvement was, initially, slow.[35]

Table 7.4. Percentage Passes, 1985–1987

Year	Sat	Passed	% Pass
1985	71	18	25.4
1986	90	14	15.8
1987	107	18	16.8

Source: Annual Reports 1985–87.

Nevertheless, the percentage of passes showed a stronger upward movement between 1990 and 1994.

Table 7.5. Percentage Passes, 1990–1994

Year	June	December	Total
1990	17	19	36
1991	27	24	51
1992	25	22	47
1993	25	17	42
1994	9	40	49

Source: Annual Report 1995, 14.

In 2000, ninety-five students succeeded in the June and December examination sittings.[36] The increased number of passes was partly a function of the role of the consortium, and partly a result of the significant increase in student intake.

There was a significant increase in the number of graduates during the 1990s. In the years after 1987, the records do not enable a comparison of students sitting as opposed to students passing. However, there was an increase from thirty-six graduates in 1990 to seventy-nine in 1997.

The training school's success was probably attributable to improved teaching methodology in the form of tutorials and team work; the consortium's ability, partly through its links with London, to keep up with changes in the ACCA syllabuses; the embracing of methodologies consistent with modern technology; and the introduction of the "Student Training Record" (STR), by which students were expected to keep a portfolio of their experiences. The consortium also included non-audit firm students, who paid higher fees. Following changes in the syllabus in the early 1990s and in December 2001, the study school received additional funding from the United Kingdom. "This assistance helped to bring about a significant expansion of student intake. Some subjects had over 100 student participants."[37] The success continued, peaking at 151 graduates in 2007.

Both the study school and the consortium went into decline and collapsed by 2016, mainly because the audit firms and the ACCA ceased their contributions to the consortium. One final factor was that the consortium, rightly or wrongly, believed that the ICAJ was seeking to "control" the organization.[38]

Table 7.6. ACCA (Professional Graduates) at Three-Year Intervals, 2001–2016

2001	91
2004	130
2007	151
2010	60
2013	69
2016	100

Source: Annual Reports 2001–16.

The number of passes in the professional examination, having increased substantially up to 2007, declined by 23 per cent over the period 2001 to 2016. The fall could be attributed, in part, to a 28 per cent decline in student intake between 2001 and 2016. The idea that the fall was partly a result of a declining demand for accountants[39] was scoffed at by two of the author's interviewees who, though admitting that Jamaica's failure rate was the highest in the Caribbean, did not see accountancy as a dead-end for employment.[40] The decline may have been attributable, in part, to conceptual changes in the 2007 syllabus of the ACCA, which had revised its examinations to fit the needs of the marketplace. The professional level of ACCA 2007 was based on skills and on the application of knowledge. The ACCA 2007 was "designed to deliver a broad-based qualification focussing on the essential skills of accounting, business, and finance. It offered a choice of examinations and work competencies to allow students and their sponsors to tailor the path of the qualification to suit their needs."[41] Others have suggested weaknesses in the Jamaican educational system and "rote learning" among the students. The relative lack of experience of students entering the profession may also be a contributing factor to the recent weaker performances. In the past, students often had experience of accounting before embarking on professional studies, so that there had been some exposure to accounting prior to capping that experience with certification. Prior experience was no longer the norm. Another factor (and perhaps the most important one) adduced to explain inadequate performance is that the level of tuition was not commensurate with the level of examinations. Tuition providers often failed to participate in ACCA updates.[42] The removal of matriculation requirements to almost zero – in contrast to the former system of inviting candidates with GCE ordinary and advanced levels – and the introduction of the mature students' admissions may also have contributed to poorer performances in the ACCA examinations.

Graduates in the ICAJ/ACCA Regular Programme fell from 164 and 130 in 2003 and 2004, respectively to sixty-six in 2005–6.[43] Concerned with the decline, the Institute held discussions with the ACCA. In 2015, these discussions involved the implementation of training and accreditation for accounting trainers rather than institutions. The president, in the annual report of 2015–16 stated: "The Institute and the ACCA have shared a long-standing partnership through a Joint Scheme Agreement in which the ICAJ mediates on behalf of students sitting examinations locally, in addition to handling their registration and all administrative queries. We, however, remain concerned about the low pass rates of our students and will be working with the ACCA to find solutions to this challenge."[44]

With respect to registration, the Institute entered an MOU with the ACCA to implement a recruitment drive in secondary schools and tertiary institutions in Jamaica.[45]

IAS and AAT

Students could opt for an accounting technician course rather than the ICAJ/ACCA. In any case, the AAT and CAT opened the door to the ACCA programme. Students registered (through the ICAJ) for the first time in December 1975 for the Institute of Accounting Staff (IAS), London, examinations. The IAS, a subsidiary of the ACCA, later merged with the Association of Technicians in Finance and Accounting, at the time a subsidiary of the CIPFA, to form the Association of Accounting Technicians (AAT). The AAT was jointly sponsored from 1980 by the ACCA and four other major chartered accountancy bodies in the United Kingdom: CIPFA, the ICAEW, CIMA and ICAS.[46] The AAT was introduced into Jamaica- the first overseas site of the examination – in 1981 as part of ACCA's partnership with other British firms. The establishment of the AAT also mirrored the decision of the ICAJ to introduce a second or lower tier of professionals. Part of the attraction of the AAT as a successor to the IAS for potential recruits was that successful completion of the course brought exemptions from Level 1 of the ACCA and was therefore a path to ACCA certification. Possession of an AAT also opened up possibilities for employment in the public sector, industry and commerce and in the offices of accounting practitioners.[47] The AAT enjoyed a long run in Jamaica, beginning in 1981. AAT students were, numerically, a significant part of the student body. There was a 42 per cent increase in admissions to the AAT between 1980 and 1988, compared to a 29 per cent increase in ACCA admissions over the same period. In the 1979–89 period 1,090 students were admitted into the AAT programme.

Table 7.7. Applications and Admissions, AAT, 1980–1989

Year	Applications	Admissions
1979/80	129	109
1980/81	n/a	145
1984/85	172	158
1986/87	388	354
1987/88	282	259
1988/89	68	65

Source: Annual Reports 1980–89.

Table 7.8. Students Recommended to Pursue ACCA and AAT, 1980–1994

Year	ACCA	AAT	Total
1979–1980	79	109	188
1980–1981	143	145	288
1985–1986	171	158	329
1986–1987	240	354	594
1987–1988	268	259	527
1990–1991	306	54	360
1993–1994	569	65	634

Source: Annual Reports 1980–94.

The AAT segment of the student population peaked at 354 in 1986–87. In 1990–91, only fifty-four students were admitted. From the 1990s onward, the numbers became erratic.

In 1988, the AAT proposed a joint examination scheme (comparable to the ICAJ/ACCA Joint Scheme). The proposal, in part, recommended that:

- The AAT (UK) examination would be adopted until local exams had been developed over a period of time.
- The AAT Jamaica Limited would have a Board of Directors to perform duties similar to the Council of ICAJ.
- "The Institute will . . . categorize and recognize the AAT as a 'second Tier Accounting Body.'"
- The AAT, UK and the ICAJ will be the two major sponsoring bodies. Institutions that have been closely associated with AAT students will be asked to be subscribers to the Memorandum and Articles of Association: These include the College of Arts Science and Technology, the Institute of Management and Production (IMP) and Duff's Business College Limited.[48]

The deliberate marketing efforts of the AAT to boost interest in the examination enjoyed temporary success. There was, in Jamaica, a council of the AAT that met on a monthly basis, but the AAT (UK) decided against a Joint Examination Scheme until a local secretariat was established.[49] However, in 1993, 1994, 1995 and again in 1999, 2001 and 2006, AAT representatives visited

Jamaica to update the Council on their evaluation schemes; to encourage the development of an overseas branch in Jamaica; to foster employers' interest in the new evaluation scheme; and to enhance the relationship between ICAJ and AAT UK, whereby the ICAJ would undertake certain administrative functions for the AAT in Jamaica.[50]

The ICAJ continued to play an administrative role with respect to the AAT students. The marketing of the AAT sometimes bore fruit, and numbers rose to 1,166 in 2001–2.[51] The numbers fell to 513 in 2007–8. There is, therefore, a correlation between the temporary rise of AAT numbers and AAT London's marketing strategies. Up to 2005–6 the ICAJ continued to provide administrative support for 704 AAT students and in 2007–8, 513 AAT students. However, the applications continued to fall. A report in February 2008 noted that most of the centres that carried the AAT programme no longer offered AAT support.[52]

It is apparent that with the introduction of CAT in 1997, the AAT ran its course in Jamaica. However, there were other factors involved with the gradual decline of the AAT – a decline that began before the introduction of CAT. One source claimed that the AAT required employers to oversee students' training, and some employers were more interested in keeping persons at student level to get work done and to remain perpetually as students.[53] Ultimately, it was the rise of CAT by the ACCA that delivered the final blow to the AAT.

CAT: Certified Accounting Technician

The erosion of AAT quickened when the ACCA withdrew from the joint sponsorship of the AAT and established in 1997 the competing Certified Accounting Technician (CAT) programme. The CAT, entirely controlled by the ACCA, was intended to complement the ACCA's own international business structure. The CAT was, like the ICAJ/ACCA, a joint examination scheme of the Institute and the ACCA. Although a second-tier examination, the CAT, like the AAT, provided an opening for second-tier professionals to move towards the top-tier ACCA.

The certified accounting technician became paramount. The following table demonstrates the decline of the AAT and the rise of ACCA's CAT.

Table 7.9. AAT and CAT, 2000–2006

Year	ACCA	AAT	CAT
1999–2000	1,800	n/a	1,472
2000–2001	1,960	(230)	1,751
2001–2002	2,134	1,166	1,735
2002–2003	2,458	1,147	1,850
2003–2004	2,471	785	1,893
2004–2005	2,557	n/a	1,900
2005–2006	2,865	704	1,852

Source: Annual Reports 2000–2006.

There is little doubt that the decline in the number of AAT students is mostly attributable to the introduction of the CAT, which was the ACCA's competing second-tier examination. The CAT, introduced in 1997, grew rapidly and largely at the expense of the AAT. Official visits of AAT representatives for negotiations with the ICAJ to promote AAT led to occasional upswings in AAT, but were unable to stem the decline to 513 by 2008. The Overseas Examinations Commission, in its 2008–9 report, confirmed the slide in AAT examination entries: "While ACCA numbers are rising, registration for the Association of Accounting Technicians (AAT) has been declining steadily since ACCA's introduction of the CAT qualification."[54] Between 2000 and 2006 there was a 59 per cent increase in registered ICAJ/ ACCA students and a 26 per cent increase in CAT students. At UWI Career Expos high school students proved particularly interested in the new CAT programme.

Entry for CAT was restricted to Jamaican nationals or persons ordinarily resident in Jamaica. CAT students as a percentage of the total student population rose quickly from 25 per cent in 1998– 99 to 37.5 per cent in 1999–2000. In 2000, 820 students were registered for CAT. The following table indicates the progress of CAT between 2005 and 2016.

Table 7.10. CAT Registrations Compared with ACCA, 2004–2016

Year	ACCA	CAT	Total
2004–2005	2,903	1,900	4,803
2006–2007	3,294	1,776	5,070
2008–2009	3,155	1,724	4,879
2010–2011	2,832	1,530	4,576
2012–2013	2,665	1,293	3,958
2014–2015	2,437	973	3,410
2015–2016	2,163	920	3,083

Source: Annual Reports 2005–16.

Table 7.11. CAT Registrations at Two-Year Intervals, 2000–2015

2000	2001	2003	2005	2007	2009	2011	2013	2015
820	1,751	1,850	1,900	1,699	1,724	1,530	1,293	973

Source: Annual Reports 2000–2016.

The Institute would have been happy with the number of students graduating from the CAT programme between 2001 and 2007, but the number of passes fell significantly between 2008 and 2015, primarily perhaps because of the introduction by the ACCA of the Foundations in Accountancy (FIA), which gradually overtook CAT.

Table 7.12. CAT Passes, 2001–2015

2001	2003	2005	2007	2009	2011	2013	2015
145	180	170	120	70	35	15	7

Source: Annual Reports 2001–15.

Foundations in Accountancy (FIA)

The FIA reflected the new "open access" policy of the ACCA route to ACCA certification. The Foundations in Accountancy (FIA) was another joint scheme between the ICAJ and ACCA, which was examined for the first time in 2011. The scheme was referred to as the FIA Joint Scheme (JS). It consisted of an introductory Certificate in Financial and Management Accounting, Diploma in Accounting and Business, and the Certified Accounting Technicians (CAT) Qualifications.[55] No specific matriculation requirements were necessary. There were, however, "self-check" modules in English and mathematics to enable potential candidates to "check" their competencies in these areas and to improve them as necessary.[56] The FIA was designed to provide "flexible" entry points with certification at each level. In theory, the FIA opened opportunities to students who, though committed to qualifying themselves, did not have the generally accepted educational background or an adequate learning environment.

All students who successfully complete nine examinations of the FIA/JS, the Foundations in Professionalism module, twelve months' work experience and performance objectives shall be deemed to have satisfied the examination requirements of both the ACCA and ICAJ and shall be eligible to apply for the designation Certified Accounting Technician of both bodies. All students who successfully complete the Diploma in Accounting and Business via the Foundation Level routes can be transferred directly to the ACCA Joint Scheme based on the ACCA Qualification at the Fundamental Skills Level.[57]

Lowering the levels of matriculation increased the pool of students but would hardly have contributed to improved performance. The FIA students, in fact, were responsible for an increasing number of dropouts.

THE MSER

The ACCA created a new entry route for mature (over twenty-one) students. The intention was to expand the student body and to create opportunities for mature Jamaicans who had practical experience but were weak on formal academic qualifications. Some members of ICAJ were always opposed to MSER, whose pass rate was low.[58]

The MSER Scheme allowed students to sit two papers – 1.1 Accounting and 1.2 Cost and Management Accounting 1. Students who succeeded in those papers, within the time limit, were automatically transferred to the student registers of the ICAJ and ACCA.

Table 7.13. MSER Entries, 2001–2008

2001	2002	2004	2005	2007	2008
255	327	292	309	288	231

Source: Annual Reports 2001–8.

Fees

Working with and for students was to the mutual advantage of students (certification) and Institute (operational expenses). The ACCA shifted from a "flat rate" payment to a four-tiered system.

Table 7.14. Fees, 2016

Band	No. of Students	Fees per Student
A	1–250	£7.00
B	251–500	£6.00
C	501–1,000	£5.00
D	1,001–2,500	£4.00
E	2,501 +	£3.00

Source: Service Order, 23 September 2016.

The Institute's role as agent of the ACCA required, in deference to ACCA rules, registration and receiving student payments that were dispatched to ACCA. Students registered under the joint scheme "shall pay their annual subscriptions due to the Institute directly to the Institute". The ICAJ will receive "in recognition of the work undertaken by ICAJ for JES" £3 per registered student.[59]

Students paid a fee that covered registration with the Institute and the ACCA. The increase in fees was often related to the steady depreciation of the Jamaican dollar from almost J$1:1USD in the early 1970s to, in contemporary times, USD$1: J$128 and inflation (at the time of writing). The sterling conversion rate looked even more formidable than the US dollar conversion.

Table 7.15. Students' Fees, 1995–2008

Year	Annual Subscriptions	Registration Fee
1995–1997	$800	$800
1997–1998	$1,200	$800
1998/99	$1,500	$1,000
1999/2000	$2,000	$1,500
2008	$2,200	$1,650

Source: Annual Reports 1995–2008.

In 1997–98 a "re-registration fee" of $2,000 was introduced, which rose to $2,500 in 1998–99. Late payment fees rose from $1,200 to $1,500 between 1998 and 1999.[60] Fees were to prove a consistent challenge to students.

Computer-Based Examinations

Computer literacy became a part of administration, registration, payment of fees and examinations. Initially, students had the option of sitting on-line or paper-based examinations.[61] Moreover, if they desired to sit on-line examinations, they could register at any time of the year. The Overseas Examinations Commission, which had established by 2009 a computer lab examination room accommodating forty-two candidates at a time, was licensed to proctor such examinations.[62] Examinations were offered four times per year in place of the usual June and December examinations.[63] In 2009, another change in examination methods took place. The advanced level papers of the CAT introduced multiple-choice questions (MCQS) (objective tests), and the pass mark was increased from 40 to 50 per cent.

Portability of Certification

It can be argued that the ICAJ's association with the ACCA, which was global in its reach, as well as the phenomenon of "globalization" from at least the 1980s and the establishment of the WTO and GATS after 1995, encouraged students to consider seriously the portability of their certificates. Although accounting bodies competed with each other, portability was facilitated by cooperation between them.

Migration is generally directed to the North American continent. However, Jamaican accountants have migrated to English-speaking New Zealand and also to non-English-speaking Europe. Overseas Jamaican accountants have a commendable reputation for good performance. At home, the performance of the MSc graduates has been impressive.[64] On the flip side of the emigration of Jamaican accountants is the immigration into Jamaica of overseas accountants. The hotel industry, for example, has been recruiting its own nationals to service the industry.

Through the years, the partnership between the ICAJ and the ACCA remained unchallenged, for the most part. The two organizations are separate, and competitive relations are modified by collaboration.[65] In the late 1990s, however, perhaps partly because of the predominant position of the United States in international business and partly because of the direction of Jamaican emigrant outflows, students began to challenge ACCA dominance in Jamaica. Their perception was, first, that ACCA or ICAJ membership was not as attractive as the US-based CPA. The argument against the ACCA was that it was "potentially obsolescent in the market-place of the future".[66] At expositions and orientation sessions students questioned the marketability of the ACCA as a qualification in the global environment. Second, the US-based CPA was more flexible since, with that certification, employment in either Jamaica or the United States was possible. Third, it was becoming challenging for Jamaicans with ACCAs to be accepted in the US market since a growing number of states were refusing to recognize the ACCA graduate as a sufficient qualification for the CPA.[67] However, the CPA opened the door to Caribbean nationals to practise in Georgia, California, Delaware and New Jersey.[68]

In response to the rising number of queries on the CPA as an alternative entry route to the profession, the Council took the principled position that it had an obligation to provide its students with information on all routes of entry.[69] In an earlier chapter it was noted that the ICAJ had opened its doors to the CPA and the CGA of Canada. Immediate past president Raphael Gordon, in his weekly column published in the *Daily Gleaner*, highlighted one particular advantage of the ACCA: "The ACCA syllabus had been adopted by the United Nations, as the benchmark for a global curriculum."[70] This explanation was a bit misleading.[71] The enthusiasm for the US-based CPA had, in fact, emerged strongly among MSc graduates ever since the 1980s.[72] While each state of the United States was responsible for admitting, examining and certifying students, "in practice, all states sat the same examination, the uniform CPA examination run by the AICPA. Success in that examination enabled the candidate to apply to the state association to be licensed."[73]

The US-based CPA has been received with more enthusiasm by Jamaican students than Canada's CGA. However, the Canadian CGA was also an attractive prospect for many potential young Jamaican accountants.[74] Canada's CGA was regarded as an "Innovative Option to Achieve Our Career Goal". A letter to the newsletter editor illustrates the impact of globalization of the profession on potential accounting students. The correspondent wrote: "Arising from my plans to relocate to Canada, I began the search for a well-recognized program of study that offers the flexibility of distance education." Moreover, "most recently, CGA Canada has entered into a mutual recognition agreement with the ACCA, which, essentially, provides a mechanism for members to become designated by the other association. This, I believe, is very exciting and reflects the growing globalization of our profession."[75]

The Canadian "express entry" programme encouraged highly skilled Jamaican professionals, in areas such as health care, financial services and construction to apply for entry to Canada.[76]

The CSME notwithstanding, movement within the Caribbean was difficult.[77] The preference of Jamaican students for North America was based on the rational reconciliation of education with opportunity. Education, portability of certification and emigration merged. Globalization did not always constitute a disadvantage.

Chapter 8

The ICAJ Today

The ICAJ emerged from the Jamaican financial crisis of the late 1990s in a much stronger legal position to enforce regulations governing the licensing of practitioners. This was a solution to a problem first identified at least from the late 1970s. The credibility of the organization was deepened by the general agreement between the ICAJ, the PAB and the Ministry of Finance that international standards would be the norm by which professional accountancy would be judged in Jamaica, in both the private and public sectors. The CPE/CPD programme, no longer confined to members of the Institute, broadened participation to include the general body of accountants.

The increased workload of the Institute was eased both by the continuous physical expansion of the Ruthven Road headquarters and by expansion of the secretariat. Customer service was treated with some urgency. A renewed expansion phase, which began after 2009 under the regime of Archibald Campbell (2009–11), continued into the regimes of Vintoria Bernard (2011–13) and Dennis Chung (2013–15). The new and modern two-storey building, with its meticulously kept grounds and car park, has ensured that the original 1980 building is barely a memory. The expansion of the headquarters included the construction of a caretaker's cottage.[1]

The Secretariat

The growth of the secretariat is a measure of the expansion of the Institute itself. The secretariat staff increased from four or five persons in 1978 to thirteen in 2000.[2] With the expansion of the secretariat, staff welfare became a more urgent priority. The Institute introduced a contributory pension scheme in March 1999 for its employees. The scheme grew from J$94,000 in 2000 to J$617,000 in 2014. Salaries and related expenses approached J$19 million in 2014. Employee benefits reached nearly J$21 million in 2014.

Table 8.1. The ICAJ Secretariat

Year	Income	Expenditure
1987	$276,904	$271,281
1988	$371,241	$410,143
1994	$1,720,538	$1,756,953
1995	$4,813,619	$3,932,728

Source: Annual Reports 1987, 1988, 1994 and 1995.

Membership

The steady rise in membership of the Institute over the years is a testimony both to the reputation of the organization and to marketing strategies pursued by the Institute from time to time.

It would be erroneous to think that the Institute did not face challenges with respect to membership, one of the main financial columns of the Institute. The membership of the ICAJ, for example, had stagnated by the first two years of the twenty-first century. Graduating students, who constitute a major market for membership of the ICAJ, were not seeking membership. The number of graduates increased more rapidly than membership, leaving the Institute with the challenge of persuading qualified non-members to join the ICAJ. On 7 October 2000, the Institute worried that the slow rate in membership growth resulted from the growing attraction of the MBA.

Economic recession and financial hardships took their toll on student membership and directly on the output of graduates. Difficult economic times, the challenge of obtaining study leave, lack of access to internet services by some potential students, the failure rate—all conspired to reduce the number of students. In turn, the high failure rate resulted from the tendency of some teachers of accounting not to attend ACCA briefings to keep them up to date. Furthermore, ICAJ/ACCA graduates who migrated often dropped their ICAJ overseas membership in favour of membership of overseas bodies. Even then, there were noticeable resignations of overseas members who had settled into their new communities.

Membership of the ICAJ from overseas had always been welcomed by the ICAJ. There were thirty-two overseas members in 1981, a probable consequence of emigration in the immediately preceding volatile years. There were eighteen overseas members in 1991.[3] With further migration, the overseas membership of the Institute rose sharply to ninety-four in 2014–15. That figure, however, did not reveal the number of accountants who dropped their membership of the ICAJ for membership of overseas professional associations.

Migration of professionals became more visible in the early twenty-first century. Students, as we indicated in the previous chapter, looking towards their future, had become more acutely aware of the material advantage of the portability of certificates. Globalization reinforced the principle. Jamaica's net migration continued just below the emigration peak in 1980.[4] Among the migrants were scores of professionals.

The marginal increase in ICAJ membership from 743 to 756 (31 March 2003) and the resignation of twelve members in one year was a symptom of the new reality.

Distinguished Members of the Institute

The Institute recognizes Jamaicans who have contributed significantly to the development of the accounting profession and to the Institute itself.

Membership and Finances

The financial viability of the Institute is related both to the size of the student body and that of the Institute's membership. It is true that as a voluntary association, the Institute received tax concessions "under the mutuality principle".[5] Access to occasional grants from the PSOJ, the IDB, and the PAB for specific projects were not designed to cover operational expenses.

The Institute as a voluntary organization looked largely to self-financing efforts (such as interest and dividends from financial instruments – 14 per cent in 2000 – room rental, seminars, luncheons, the *Charter* magazine) to strengthen its revenue base. Other self-financing activities included continuing development sessions and the annual business conference. But membership remained one of the major columns of financial viability. The figures for 2004, 2010 and 2015 indicate that members' subscriptions and admission fees together with students' subscriptions and registration fees contributed 65, 64 and 69 per cent, respectively, to the Institute's income. This was a reduction from 81 per cent in 2000.

Membership fees, taken separately from students' subscriptions, ranged between 30 and 59 per cent of revenue from 2011 to 2015.

Table 8.2. Income from Membership

Year	Total Revenue ($000)	Income from Membership ($000)	Percentage
2010–2011	50,455	15,406	30
2011–2012	48,318	16,954	35
2012–2013	40,763	17,551	43
2013–2014	39,960	20,277	51
2014–2015	36,686	21,681	59

Source: "Five Year Statistics", Annual Report 2014–15, 28.

The membership is also essential for the "manpower" needs to sustain the activities of the current sixteen committees. The largest committee, the Taxation Committee, has had up to twenty-six members and the Public

Sector Committee twenty-five persons. It is routine for members to spread their energies over more than one committee.

However, ultimately, it is as important to keep new customers, as it is to attract them in the first place. "Our profession, like many others, continues to grapple with the challenge of attracting new members while retaining existing ones, particularly in light of economic realities that constrain our ability to meet the growing demand from members for 'value for money', while providing the highest quality service."[6]

Membership Drive

In response to slow membership growth in the first years of the twenty-first century, the Council mounted an aggressive and successful drive to raise the membership to one thousand and beyond. It increased the subvention for advertising and public relations, rising to just over J$2 million dollars in 2014, to promote membership by publicizing the advantages of membership.

The membership drive between 2006 and 2007 targeted eligible MSc, AICPA and CGA qualified persons to join the Institute. In 2006, the Council agreed to waive (temporarily) admission fees of J$6,800 for new members. The publicity succeeded in drafting forty-four new members over the year 2006–7. From a modest membership of 321 and 421 in 1981 and 1986, respectively, and 526 in 1994–95, the Institute's membership rose to 1,212 in 2016 (table 8.3).

Table 8.3. Growth of Membership at Five-Year Intervals, 1996–2016

1996	2001	2006	2011	2016
580	747	876	1,084	1,212

Source: Annual Reports 1996–2016.

Another tactic, in the early twenty-first century, was to publicize more systematically the benefits of membership. The benefits, as listed in 2015, included professional development, preferential rates for seminars, access to research and technical expertise for the solution of work-related problems, the opportunity to serve on governing boards and to contribute to national accounting development.

In 2010, another benefit was provided through a welfare fund for members. In this sense, the ICAJ began to assume some of the features of a mutual aid society. The welfare fund, financed partly by members' contributions and a 10 per cent donation from each year's surplus, offered relief from poverty, distress and illness, provided funeral grants and disaster relief for all members (past and present) of the ICAJ.[7] During the year 2012–13, the Institute made a donation of $75,000 to the fund.[8] There were two major limitations on the potential success of the welfare fund. The first was that subscriptions were not as abundant as hoped, and second, demands for assistance were substantial.[9] It is young days yet for the full development of the programme. In 2012, the ICAJ introduced a health and life insurance scheme for its members, their dependents and staff.[10] In 2016 the Institute introduced life membership for persons in "good standing for 10 consecutive years and who were at least 40 years of age".[11] The by-laws of the Institute were modified accordingly.

The Institute looked to the large number of eligible individuals who were not yet members of the ICAJ to increase membership. They succeeded in doing so, but there is a large body of potential members who have chosen not to become members of the Institute. The Institute also resorted to the recruitment of more qualified students from the high school population – in a way, a return to the 1960s and 1970s when the ICAJ recruited the most competent O- and A-level high school graduates.

The bonding of members takes place through seminars related to professional development and social interaction.

Membership and Gender

Acknowledging the contribution of women does not detract from the signal role of distinguished men who founded, shaped and advanced the profession. However, one of the significant changes in the structure of membership of the ICAJ has been the increasing number of female members. The figures from 2010 to 2016 indicate a numerical advantage in favour of female membership.

Table 8.4. Membership by Gender

Year	Total	Male	Female	% Male	% Female
2010	1,079	516	563	48	52
2011	1,085	497	588	46	54
2012	1,139	522	617	46	54
2013	1,190	541	649	45	55
2014	1,225	551	674	45	55
2015	1,234	570	664	45	55
2016	1,212	580	632	48	52

Source: Annual Reports 2010–16.

A survey of the involvement of women chairing or serving as members of the Institute's various committees indicates active female involvement, including executive directorship of the Institute. In the case of the Taxation Committee, in one year there were seventeen women as opposed to nine men. On the Future of the Profession Committee (twenty-two members), there were eleven women; on the Student Affairs Committee, there were eleven women and seven men. While three women have served as president, they have only rarely made it to the Council, the policymaking body of the ICAJ. The twelve-person Council between 2006 and 2010 averaged nine male members and three female members. This gender disparity within the Council has not gone unnoticed by former president, Patricia Hayle.[12] In the 2016–17 administration the number of women on Council went up to 50 per cent of the membership. As members of the accountancy profession in Jamaica and as members of Council, women have often played a very outstanding public role. For example, Pamela Monroe Ellis, apart from being the present auditor general of Jamaica, has also served for two terms as a board member of IFAC, chairing the governance committee of that international organization. (Bruce Scott, past president of ICAJ, served as Ellis's technical adviser.) Elaine Robinson has served as honorary secretary of the Council, and the current executive director of the Institute is Mrs Rosemarie Heaven.

Outreach and National Profile (Professional Development Clubs)

The responsibility of membership is associated with upholding the integrity of the profession and contributing to public education. Members have also been encouraged to volunteer to be part of outreach programmes. A National Outreach Sub-Committee (2007–8) directed its attention to specific areas of national development. One result was the recommendation that the Institute become a member of the National Council on Education. Members advised school bursars on "cash flow management, investment portfolio management and Microsoft Excel manipulation techniques".[13] There were other proposals recommending that members sit on school boards. Members of the Institute have served as external examiners for community colleges. Public lectures on topical issues have become part of the continuing effort of the Institute to raise its public profile.

The goal identified since the late 1970s of giving the Institute a strong public profile encouraged some new directions at the start of the twenty-first century. The new direction in professional development included writing and public speaking skills. The ICAJ established a writers' club, which in March 2012 had fifty-six members and a Toastmasters' Club in 2012.[14] The Toastmasters' Club, designed to enhance self-confidence particularly in public speaking, had, at the end of 2013, thirty-nine members, thirty-five of whom were charter members.[15] The modern marketplace requires more than technical professional skills in addressing and reporting to the board, and to some extent, research skills.[16]

ICAJ and Philanthropic Work

The ICAJ and its members have a long tradition of community and public service. Parallel to their substantive positions as chartered accountants, some members have been active as leaders in the Kiwanis and Rotary clubs, which are institutionally committed to social service. Others have served in legal aid clinics or are justices of the peace. One member, Past President Leighton McKnight, is particularly outstanding for his work among children. "McKnight who runs the Jamaican arm of PwC has devoted his life to helping children from seriously deprived homes, assisting 50 of them with education."[17] Some of his protégés are university students or graduates. The Institute adopted the Elsie Bemand Home for Girls (founded over thirty years ago by the Business and Professional Women's Club in association with the Methodist Church) and the Sunbeam Children's Home for Boys.

The ICAJ and UWI

After many twists and turns, localization of syllabuses remains a factor in ICAJ and ICAC policy. Meanwhile, the relationship between the ICAJ and the UWI has become far more accommodating, but is not, strictly speaking, linked to the original policy of indigenization. The ICAJ seemed more comfortable with an ICAJ/UWI "partnership" and with collaboration. Both the UWI and ICAJ agreed to mutual and periodical reviews of the MSc in Accounting, to ensure that the degree "meets or exceeds the appropriate international accounting education standards, such as International Education Standard (IES 4) promulgated by the International Federation of Accountants".[18] The accounting degree remained under constant review both by the UWI and by the ICAJ "to ensure comparability with the leading academic programmes in the United States and the United Kingdom, incorporating recent changes in the curricula of the professional programmes in the US and the UK, and account for the changing needs of Jamaica and the region with respect to the role of accounting in the economic development of the region".[19] In 2014–15 the ICAJ discussed the possibility of "creating a pathway for UWI accounting students to obtain an ACCA qualification while earning their undergraduate degree; and in conjunction with ACCA's accreditation of the UWI Mona campus to facilitate an easier and more programmed transition from UWI undergraduate programmes into ACCA – similar to UWI's Cave Hill and St Augustine campuses".[20]

In September 2005, the Mona School of Business and Management introduced a part-time MSc degree in accounting.[21] Students flocked to the part-time programme, no doubt because of the students' financial challenges in a job-scarce economy in which an increasing number of students had to work and study. The ICAJ, committed to ensuring the continuation of the MSc full-time programme, offered a scholarship, valued at J$744,000, for a full-time MSc (accounting) student.

In 2004–5, there were 124 BSc Accounting, 23 MSc Accounting graduates, and 50 master's students on register.[22] In 2006–7 there were 43 BSc and 14 MSc graduates. Registration for 2006 consisted of 84 undergraduates (accounting) and 136 in the graduate programme. There were twenty-six full-time and forty part-time faculty in 2004.

As the ICAJ and the UWI moved more closely together, there were two further developments between 2000 and 2015. The first was a cooperative agreement between UWI and ICAJ to develop a three-month internship programme for MSc (full-time) and BSc students. Such an internship was long overdue and had certainly been advocated since 1988. Two firms, Ernst and Young (in particular) and Price Waterhouse, facilitated the internship financially, since some internships (which provided a work experience in an audit environment) necessitated overseas travel and residential costs. Council encouraged its members to support the internship programme by admitting students to their offices.[23] The Department of Management Studies reported favourably on the internship programme.[24]

A second agreement between the Mona School of Business and Management (MSBM, UWI) and ICAJ was that MSc accounting students would register with the ICAJ in exchange for a payment by MSBM to the ICAJ of an annual membership fee for each eligible MSc accounting student for two consecutive years, starting 1 October 2015. In other words, MSc students would be registered with the ICAJ. Thus, the recommendation made as far back as the 1970s to incorporate UWI students into the ICAJ had been virtually fulfilled. Much had happened and changed to enable the new dispensation. The ICAJ now speaks of "leveraging" the research capacity of the UWI in the same breath as promoting an ICAJ Brand. Meanwhile, the ICAJ continues to believe that continued collaboration with the ACCA is of benefit to the profession.

The ICAJ resumed the old discussion with UWI of variant papers in Jamaican law and taxation as an alternative to the current UK Law and Taxation papers taken by students as part of the ICAJ/ACCA joint examination scheme. UWI teaches an MA course in taxation. To this extent indigenization remains, but only as a rather distant sub-theme. The ICAJ proposed, in August 2015, the marketing ("to a greater extent") of the UWI Mona MSc Accounting programme as its own local qualification. Gone is the notion of the ICAJ as a "potential examining body". But the idea that "We are seeking to leverage UWI's education infrastructure" has concealed in it both the distant memory of indigenization and the newer vision of collaboration.[25]

Meanwhile, UWI scheduled its 2015 academic programme to enable students to qualify as chartered accountants within two years after graduating from the BSc Accounting programme. The ICAJ's commitment to UWI's MSc is evident in the joint offer by ICAJ and the UWI of a fiftieth anniversary (2015) postgraduate scholarship. Perhaps, the professional and the academic are finally meeting. Abroad, the ACCA worked closely with the University of London on an "integrated Master's programme in Professional Accountancy".[26] The Canadian CGA certification required a first degree.

From its simple foundations in 1965, the ICAJ has become a rather complex organization. It is at once an educational institution; a lobby group of accountants who have played a leading role in public education on business and finance; a technical adviser to government; and a determined and successful advocate of accountancy as a profession in Jamaica.

8.1 ICAJ Headquarters today

8.2 The Secretariat of the ICAJ 2016. In front, Rosemarie Heaven, executive director, ICAJ.

Philmore Ogle – 2005

Jasper Burnett – 2006

Kenneth Lewis – 2007

Raphael Gordon – 2008

Compton Rodney – 2009

Donald Reynolds – 2010

Richard Downer – 2011

Denis Goldson – 2012

Everton McDonald – 2013

Eric Crawford – 2014

Donald Wehby – 2015

Earl Jarrett – 2016

8.3 Distinguished members of the Institute

8.4 Guests at ICAJ Golden Awards gala

8.5 ICAJ Council, 2016

8.6 Celebrating the fiftieth anniversary of the Institute

8.7 ICAJ and UWI cooperation agreement. Seated at centre, Pro-Vice Chancellor Professor Kenneth Hall, principal of the Mona campus.

Conclusion

The decision to establish the ICAJ in 1965 was prompted partly by a nationalistic reaction against the dominant position of British expatriate accountants in Jamaica and the consequent exclusion of Jamaicans from the accountancy profession. The Institute's early activities were, therefore, determined partly by the urge to reduce the marginalization of Jamaicans in the accountancy profession by initiating a training programme for Jamaican accountants to fill the estimated three hundred potential vacancies in the island.

The history of the ICAJ illustrates the impact of the national and international environment on the structure and operations of a national organization. The partnership with the ACCA was intended to be a first step, or an apprenticeship, for the training of Jamaican chartered accountants with international standards in mind. The association with the ACCA has proved durable.

The methodology of accountancy was moving towards the internationalization of the profession at least from the 1950s. The initial commitment to indigenization became subsumed under the demands of internationalism in the accountancy profession. Internationalism became more fundamental to the functioning of the Institute in the twenty-first century.

At the time of independence in 1962, Jamaica was caught between the expanding North American informal empire and the declining British Empire of which it had been a part since the seventeenth century. The post–World War II international economy was dominated by US capital and influence. Jamaica, with its expanding aviation, tourism and bauxite/alumina sectors, and its growing commerce with the United States, tightened its commercial links with the latter. Although US accounting practices were introduced into the island, it is entirely possible that the non-antagonistic push for Jamaican independence from the United Kingdom ensured that anglophile loyalties (ACCA) predominated over US influences (AICPA) in accountancy.

The year 1962 is important for two interrelated events – the end of the West Indies Federation (1958–62) and the proclamation of independence by two Caribbean territories, Jamaica and Trinidad and Tobago. Remaining members of the collapsed federation followed Jamaica and Trinidad and Tobago in the late 1960s and 1970s. Traditional commitments to Caribbean integration, however, promoted the concept of functional cooperation in the Caribbean region. Discussions of a regional examination body – the Caribbean Examinations Council (CXC) – started in 1964 and culminated in the first CXC examinations in 1979. CARIFTA and CARICOM, the Grand Anse Declaration and, eventually, the CSME kept regionalism alive. The accounting fraternity in the Caribbean, influenced by regionalism, proposed a regional body of accountants. The presence of the regional UCWI/UWI, opened since 1948, prompted Jamaican agitators to indigenize the local profession and to persuade the UCWI/UWI to become a part of the new frontier of opportunities for Jamaicans and other Caribbean citizens to become chartered accountants. The future of accountancy appeared bound to the Caribbean Single Market and Economy from the Grand Anse Declaration of 1989 to the Revised Treaty of Chaguaramas in 2002. Caribbean cooperation has remained an ideal. The Caribbean, apparently, has the wish, but not the will, to integrate, even at a functional level.

The Institute was established, also, at precisely the time when there was a more concerted effort to harmonize international accountancy practices. This movement towards harmonization, already evident in the 1960s, bloomed fully towards the end of the twentieth century. The international dimension is particularly important for the Institute, which had chosen the powerful and wealthy UK-based ACCA as its partner and mentor. It was an international business whose arms embraced the British Empire and Commonwealth and pulled the Jamaican Institute into the mainstream of international accountancy. In most respects, the alliance with the ACCA, which has endured, and perhaps represents a source of stability, growth and policy-making (for the most part) for the Institute, corresponds to the very conservative framework within which Jamaica greeted political independence in 1962. For all the control that the ACCA may have had over British ex-colonial territories, and the mentorship role it has played with respect to the Jamaican-based

Institute, it has also been subject to the whims of the international economy, the WTO, GATS and the increasing international integration of accountancy procedures. The ACCA, itself, while willing to work with other accounting bodies, can go its own way in international competition. The ICAJ has, almost always, followed the path of collaboration with the ACCA.

Some members of the Institute acknowledge the enormous contribution of the ACCA to the development of the Institute. Dissenting authors have seen the Institute/ACCA connection as a continuation of British colonialism, a continuation buttressed by the cooperation of powerful interest groups within the Institute itself. At the same time, it is always useful to bear in mind that the immediate goal of the founders of the Institute was to create a body of Jamaican accountants in a society that had been dominated by British expatriate accountants. International institutions such as the International Federation of Accountants (IFAC) also had a substantial impact on the internationalization of the Institute and on the accounting profession in Jamaica.

Through its brief history, the Institute has balanced its commitment to training of Jamaican accountants – arguably the key issue in the Institute's foundation – with the larger role of educating the public on economic and financial issues. Within a few years after its establishment, the Institute increasingly adopted the role of adviser to government. The changing features of the ICAJ are mirrored in the realities that, by the late twentieth century, accountants, no longer confined to specialization in financial matters, contributed to policy- and decision-making.

This study is, in part, a contribution to the history of voluntary organizations in Jamaica, whose role is, unfortunately, generally underestimated. The ICAJ is a voluntary, self-financing association of chartered accountants, which over a half century has created and nurtured a relatively successful financial and educational institution, notwithstanding challenging economic and financial circumstances. The Institute does not belong to the scores of philanthropic or welfare associations in Jamaica, although it makes its own philanthropic contributions to two children's homes. Insofar as the Institute, in more recent times, has created a welfare scheme for its members, it even bears features of a mutual aid society.

This history has been written with the recognition that an alliance between accountancy and business is inevitable. The concrete manifestation of this orientation lies in the growth of a strong alliance between the ICAJ and the

PSOJ. This alliance can become, for ideological reasons, an issue, such as during the 1970s to about 1990, a period marked both by political and economic volatility. It raises the question of the extent to which an organization whose viability rests upon its particular technical expertise can work with or resist the influence of political ideology. Yet, from the 1980s, there was a more general convergence of the ideological positions of government and Institute. Both were committed to the creation of an economic climate that favoured foreign direct investment and a business-driven ideology.

The ICAJ's journey was not confined to the technicalities of an evolving profession. Forensic accounting, which moves the contemporary accountant into areas such as industrial espionage, business intelligence gathering and due diligence enquiries, security engineering, intellectual property infringement, dispute resolution, fraud and risk management have become part of the accountant's tool kit. International concerns such as environmental accounting and money laundering, arising out of rapid globalization, have broadened the role of accountants. Through elaborate international Codes of Ethics, accountants have virtually become moral guardians of the public interest, rather than mere defenders of the interest of the firms that they audit.

The main achievement of the Institute of Chartered Accountants of Jamaica is that it effectively spearheaded the growth of accountancy in Jamaica by facilitating the studies of hundreds of Jamaican student accountants. Even now, it remains possible that there may be a pragmatic indigenization within the larger internationalist framework.

Appendix 1

Profiles of Past Presidents

1. William Thwaites, CD, FCA (1965–68)

William A. Thwaites was one of the twenty founding fathers and the first president of the ICAJ. Thwaites followed his father's footsteps in the accountancy profession in early 1941 when he joined the firm Wood, Costa and Harty. He took up articles in England in 1947 and in 1951 qualified as a chartered accountant. On his return to Jamaica, he managed the merger of Tapley Bowman and Peat Marwick Mitchell in 1958 when he assumed the position of joint senior partner. His commitment to the development of skills at Peat Marwick Mitchell, now KPMG Peat Marwick, and to the benefit of his clients, saw the growth of his firm in Jamaica with offices in Kingston and Montego Bay. A keen sportsman, he was dedicated to yachting, fishing and bird shooting. He received the Order of Distinction for excellence in the field of accountancy. Following his retirement, he undertook several directorships and consultancies.

2. Philmore Ogle, OD, FCA, FCCA (1968–70)

Philmore Ogle, a graduate of St George's College, completed his ACCA while working at the Auditor General's Department. A member of the agitating group referred to as the "Young Turks", Ogle was one of the founding fathers of the ICAJ. He was the last president of the Accountants Association of Jamaica (1958–65), which preceded the ICAJ. Ogle, the second president of the ICAJ, served in that capacity between 1968 and 1970. He was audit partner at Deloitte and Touche and subsequently headed that firm's management consulting function for about twenty years. In 2005, the UWI recognized him for "Conceptualizing and Advocating the Development of the MSc Accounting Programme". He served on the boards of the Agricultural Marketing Corporation, the Jamaica Development Bank, the National Development Bank, the Divestment Committee of the 1980s and the Public Accountancy Board. Ogle served as president of the Jamaica Chamber of Commerce between 1993 and 1995. He chaired the Investigation and Disciplinary Committees of the ICAJ. He received the Order of Distinction (Officer Class). In 2005 he was the first recipient of the Institute's Distinguished Member Award.

3. James Frederick Leigh Lord, FCA (1970–71)

James Lord served as ICAJ president 1970–1971 and vice-president of the PAB (1970–1972). Mr. Lord was one of the pioneers and founding members of the ICAJ. With dignity and zeal, he served the profession. During his term on the Council, the ICAJ achieved a new level of competence and sophistication. Always forthright and fearless in expressing his views, he gave impetus to the Council.

4. Uriel Salmon, FCA, ACCA, LLB (1971–73)

A graduate of Jericho Elementary School and Rusea's High School, Salmon had a deep yearning to be an accountant, in spite of an awareness that Jamaicans, particularly black Jamaicans, had only limited opportunities in the accounting field in Jamaica. Prior to his studies in accountancy in the United Kingdom, he was employed at the Revenue Office at Lucea and at the Audit Department. To fulfil his wish to be an accountant, he did a correspondence course, attended night school, and finally, with the help of a government scholarship, he studied in the United Kingdom. Following a brief stint at Touche Ross Thorburn, he was employed at the UWI where he served as head of the Department of Management Studies and senior lecturer in accounting and law for over twenty-five years. He was among the group of local accountants who advocated the introduction of the undergraduate and post-graduate programmes in accountancy at UWI, Mona.

As a member of the ICAJ and head of the Department of Management Studies, he was deeply committed to providing accountancy training for Jamaicans who wished to obtain qualifications in accountancy. His chairmanship of the Students and Examination Committee saw a significant increase in the ICAJ's student body. He was also moderator and external examiner for the UTECH business education programme, and vice-president of the PAB from 1972 to 1983. At the national level he served on the Parliamentary Integrity Commission from 1978 to 2004 and was vice-chairman of the board of Blue Cross of Jamaica.

5. Edgar C. Jones (1973–74)

Edgar Jones, following his graduation from Kingston Technical School, worked in the government service, including at the Income Tax Department. He became a chartered accountant in 1965. In association with J. Anthony Capleton, he founded the firm Capleton, Jones and Company, Chartered Accountants, of which he was Managing Partner. He was a founding member of the ICAJ and served on the Admissions and the Investigations Committees prior to becoming president in 1973. Active in several areas of public service, he served on the boards of the Public Passenger Transport, Jamaica Racing Commission, Prices Commission, Jamaica Commodity Trading Company and State Trading Corporation. He was a member of the Parliamentary Integrity Commission, and of the PAB.

6. Alastair MacBeath (1974–76)

Born in Perth, Scotland, Alastair MacBeath graduated with an MA in 1956 and LLB in 1958 from the University of Edinburgh. He passed the final examination of the Institute of Chartered Accountants of Scotland in May 1960, having served his apprenticeship with an Edinburgh firm. MacBeath came to Jamaica in 1960 as senior accountant at Peat Marwick Mitchell and rose to senior partner between 1968 and 1974. He served as group financial director and company secretary of the Pan-Jamaican Investment Trust Limited. Between 1977 and 1979, he was international finance director and secretary of the Island Records Group's Bahamian holding company. He was group financial director and company secretary of Rothman's International. He was chief executive officer of Carreras Group Limited (1981–86). Alastair McBeath served as senior accountant at KPMG for over ten years.

He was part-time lecturer at CAST (1961–72) in ACCA accounting subjects and part-time lecturer at the Norman Manley Law School, UWI, Mona. He served on ICAJ's Council between 1972 and 1977. He served on the PAB from 1973 to 1977. He was a member of the Rotary Club of Kingston and served on the PSOJ's Corporate Governance Committee. He was a member of ICAJ's Taxation Committee.

7. Dereck C. Sale, FCA (1976–77)

A graduate of St George's College, Dereck Sale studied for the accountancy profession in England. He took over his father's accounting business in 1966, and merged it with Touche, Ross Thorburn in 1968. Elected to the Council of ICAJ in 1973, he served as president between 1976 and 1977. He advocated the raising of the profile of the ICAJ, cooperation among Caribbean accountants, and conceptualized the introduction of a two-tier system in accountancy. He supported the indigenization of the profession and the need for accountants to extend their interest beyond that of the business community. He was a strong advocate of professional development seminars. In 1977, he demitted office as president of ICAJ in order to concentrate on planning and organizing the first major Caribbean Conference of Accountants, which he conceived as a catalyst for unifying the region's disparate accounting bodies. He was among those members who strongly advocated the provision of headquarters for the Institute. His article "The Gathering Storm" was published in the US *Journal of Accountancy*. He was associated with the fledgling Jamaica Stock Exchange and the PAB. He was a part-time lecturer in accounting at UWI, a Director of the Kingston Legal Aid Clinic and President of the Serra Club of Kingston. He served as governor of the South Florida District of Serra International for the period 1976–77. He migrated to Canada, where he has published fiction and non-fiction works.

8. Brian Mair, FCA (June to December 1977)

Mair's presidency lasted just a few months. As president of the ICAJ, he signed the agreement for the ICAJ to join the international Federation of Accountants in 1977. He was an ardent supporter of ICAJ/UWI cooperation in the development of the accountancy profession in Jamaica.

9. Jasper Burnett, CD, FCA, FCCA (1977–80)

Jasper Burnett had considered teaching as a career but opted to join the Jamaica Constabulary Force where he worked between 1949 and 1954, prior to his departure for the United Kingdom to study accountancy. He was an audit clerk at Brennan Parkinson in 1954–55. He has been variously associated with Price Waterhouse, Coopers and Lybrand, Touche Ross Thorburn, and his own firm Burnett, Jackson, Parkinson. He retired from partnership and from public practice in 1997.

A member of Council between 1974 and 1982, Burnett completed the term of Brian Mair who resigned unexpectedly in December 1977. His years as president are marked by the acquisition of permanent headquarters at 8 Ruthven Road. As president he also concentrated on increasing professional education, a process introduced when he organized and chaired the first seminar for Caribbean accountants on 6 July 1974. He also presided over the Caribbean Conference of Accountants in Jamaica, 20–22 April 1978. Burnett was an ardent supporter of the indigenization of the profession. His tenure saw an increase in the number of locally qualified professional accountants and the strengthening of ties with Caribbean and other international accounting bodies. Burnett became a member of the PAB in 1977 and served on the board of the PSOJ. He was founder and first editor of the *Charter* magazine. Burnett served on the Continuing Professional Education (CPE) and the Building, By-Laws and Handbook Committees and as chairman of the Investigations Committee. He prepared the brochure: "How to become a Chartered Accountant" for high school students. He edited the book *The Institute of Chartered Accountants of Jamaica: The First Twenty-Five Years, 1965–1990.*

Burnett was a charter member of the Kiwanis Club of Kingston and a vice-president of the Kiwanis Club of North St Andrew. He received the Order of Distinction (Commander Class) for his contribution to the field of accountancy. In 2006, ICAJ honoured him with the Distinguished Member Award. Burnett passed away in 2018.

10. Kenneth La Cruise, FCA, ACIS (1980–81)

La Cruise joined the Council in 1977 and served as vice-president between 1978 and 1980. Described as both laid back and assertive, La Cruise served as a member of the Public Accountancy Board, the Institute's Disciplinary Committee and chairman of the Taxation and Finance Committee. La Cruise is most noted for his contribution to the acquisition and refurbishing of the ICAJ's headquarters at 8 Ruthven Road. The decision to purchase the 8 Ruthven Road property was clearly a decision made by the Jasper Burnett-led Council by a majority vote. However, Vice-President La Cruise did a lot of the footwork in choosing and refurbishing 8 Ruthven Road. He was the first president to occupy the new headquarters in 1980. He was a senior partner in the firm Coopers and Lybrand from which he retired as managing partner. He became a member of the Board of the Jamaica Broadcasting Corporation and of the Jamaica Export Trading Company. La Cruise was employed at the UWI Bursary for some years.

11. Norman Adam, 1981–83

Norman Adam was a partner at KPMG for fifteen years and was honorary secretary of the Institute for over a decade.

12. Kenneth Lewis, CD, FCA, FCCA (1983–85)

Kenneth Lewis became a member of the Council in 1978, elected vice-president in 1981 and president 1983–85. He also served on several council committees and was chairman of the Audit Practices Committee. He headed the Institute's representation on the Joint Task Force formed with the Building Societies Association to consider development of the Institute's Ruthven Road property. He was senior partner in the firm Mair, Russell and Partners after 1978. He also worked with accounting firms in the United Kingdom. He received ICAJ's Distinguished Member Award in 2007.

13. Aulous Madden, OD, FCA, FCCA, FAIA (1985–87)

A graduate of St Aloysius Primary School, Aulous Madden is largely self-educated. A deeply religious man, he embarked on a correspondence course and attended extramural and evening classes at CAST and UWI. As a leader of the student society, he organized pre-examination workshops. After two years as treasurer, he was elected chairman. During his two years in this post, active membership grew from twenty-five to over two hundred. He established Aulous Madden and Company, now PKF, as a sole practitioner in 1972. He became a temporary member of the Council in 1977–78 and was elected to the Council in 1981. Appointed vice-president in 1983, he served as ICAJ's president 1985–87. As a member of Council, he served as chairman of the Students and Examination Committee for ten years, chairman of the Audit Practice Committee for five years and served on several other committees including Accounting Standards, Public Relations, Publications and CPE. He was vice-president of the PAB for thirteen years and treasurer and secretary of the PSOJ. Enthusiastic about the welfare of students, he served on the Registration and Examinations Committee. He served on Jamaica's Parliamentary Integrity Commission for nine years and was one of the first three commissioners with the Fair Trading Commission in its first three years. Madden was the founding president of ICAC and served for seven years in that capacity. As the first president of ICAC, Madden saw the main issues facing the accountancy profession in the Caribbean as the establishment of indigenous qualifications with regional and international acceptance and recognition; writing and publication of texts on Caribbean law, taxation, accounting and finance; and the removal of regulations that currently restrict accountants from one territory in the region from practising in another. Madden was the first Caribbean chartered accountant to be appointed to the ACCA Council. He created history when in 1996 he was elected the first ACCA Council member from the Western world. Aulous Madden was re-elected to the ACCA

Assembly in 1999. He was the first Caribbean chartered accountant to have been so honoured.

14. Donald Reynolds, FCA, FCA (UK) (1987–89)

Donald R Reynolds, a graduate of Excelsior College and former teacher at Meadowbrook High School, enjoys the distinction of being the first UWI graduate to become president of the ICAJ, having graduated from UWI in 1965 with a BSc Econ. He completed his professional Accounting examination in 1970 and was first elected to the Council in 1981–82. He served on the Council for eighteen years. Prior to becoming vice-president in 1985, Reynolds served as a member of the Accounting Standards Committee and chairman of the Continuing Professional Education Committee. He was president of the St Andrew High School PTA and Director of the Mel Nathan Institute for Development and Social Research. The launch of the ICAC took place during Reynolds's regime. Reynolds, whose career included a stint at Touche Ross, was the recipient of ICAJ's Distinguished Member Award in 2010.

15. Everton McDonald, FCA, FCCA, BSc (1989–91)

Everton McDonald graduated with a UWI BSc (Econ) in 1969 and received his ACCA (CACA) qualification in 1972. As a member of the ICAJ, he served as chairman of the By-Laws and Handbook Committee and advertising manager for the *Charter* magazine. He was elected to Council in 1983. He served as a member of the PAB for a number of years. He was a managing partner and territory senior partner at PricewaterhouseCoopers and was the founding chairman of PricewaterhouseCoopers Caribbean and Bermuda. He received the ICAJ's Distinguished Member Award in 2013.

16. Lancelot "Lanny" Reynolds, CD, FCA, FCCA (1991–93)

Lanny Reynolds started his career as payroll clerk with Jamaica Omnibus Services and continued as an employee at Deloitte and Touche Chartered Accountants, where he became a managing partner in 1973. He joined the staff of Jamaica National Building Society as Financial Controller, moving up to assistant general manager, and then general manager. He spent twenty-six years there. He played an essential role in the financing of the purchase of 8 Ruthven Road and other building projects of the ICAJ. Lanny Reynolds was appointed to Council in 1978, having served as first vice-president. A Kiwanian (Kingston), he was also deputy chairman of NEM Insurance Company (Jamaica) and director of Shaw Park Beach Hotel. As president of ICAJ, he made strong efforts to improve communication between the student body and the ICAJ.

17. Paul Desnoes, FCA, 1993–95

A graduate of St George's College, Paul Desnoes became a chartered accountant in 1979 and a fellow of the Institute in April 1985. He was second vice-president from 1990 to 1991, the first time such a post was instituted in the history of ICAJ. He was appointed vice-president in 1991–92. He served for seven years on the Council. He was co-chairman of the Institute's Future of the Profession Committee, on matters related to the AAT, of which he was a Council member, and held the position of chairman of the Student Affairs Committee (1984–1993). He received the Gold Merit Award and Key in 1972 in recognition of his eleven-year contribution to the Board of the Administrative Management Society, of which he was president in 1971–72.

His other areas of contribution extended to the Jamaica Red Cross where he held the post of treasurer general from 1985 to 1988 and was appointed honorary treasurer of the Jamaica Chamber of Commerce in October 1989. He was the managing partner in the audit firm Coopers and Lybrand. Prior to this he served the Metal Box Company in the capacity of company secretary and chief accountant, 1968–72, and the Gleaner Company, attaining the position of chief accountant 1964–65.

18. Eric Crawford, FCA, FCCA (1995–97)

A student of the year at CAST, where he was a business administration scholar, Eric Crawford became a professional accountant in 1974. He was the tax and legal services partner at PricewaterhouseCoopers. He became a member of ICAJ in 1979. He has served as chairman of the ICAJ Continuing Professional Education Comittee. Noting that almost all the founding fathers of the ICAJ were ACCA-trained accountants, Crawford concluded that the ACCA had made a unique and invaluable contribution to the development of the profession in Jamaica. He served as director of finance and administration in the Jamaica National Investment Company (now National Investment Bank) and chief internal auditor of the National Housing Trust. He was elected to the ACCA International Assembly as Jamaica's representative and served as president of the Public Accountancy Board. Eric Crawford received the 2014–15 ICAJ Distinguished Member Award.

19. Raphael Gordon, FCA, FCCA, FCMA (1997–99)

Raphael Gordon joined KPMG Peat Marwick on 1 November 1973, after over six years with British American Tobacco Company Limited. Raphael Gordon became a member of the Council in 1991 and served on the following committees: Admissions, Finance, Continuing Professional Education, Future of the Profession and Audit Practice. He served as chairman of the Company Law Reform Committee, the By-Laws and Handbook Committee, the Audit Practice Committee and the Public Relations and Publications Committee. He became a member of the PAB in 2000. He has served as a director of the ICAC, and as Jamaica's representative on the ACCA International Assembly. Gordon is a partner of both the audit firm of KPMG Peat Marwick and the consulting firm of KPMG Peat Marwick & Partners. Gordon was responsible for the audits of various manufacturing companies, statutory bodies, financial and educational institutions and has specific responsibilities for the audits of a number of companies listed on the Jamaica Stock Exchange.

He is also a member of the EDP Auditors Association, Inc. and Jamaica's lead contact in the KPMG Worldwide Banking and Finance Regulatory and International Corporate Finance Networks, a computer audit specialist and statistical audit specialist. He was the Distinguished Member Awardee in 2008.

During his regime, discussions on the revision of the company law continued, and a security fence along the northern perimeter of the property was erected. His regime saw the introduction of a pension scheme for members and staff and the completion of the refurbishing of the ICAJ library. Two major concerns emerged during his regime: the FINSAC crisis, necessitating internal review, and the inflow of overseas practitioners, arising from changes in the global marketplace.

20. C. Patricia Hayle, FCA, FCCA (1999–2001)

A graduate of Immaculate Conception High School, C. Patricia Hayle was elected to the Council in 1993. Her legacy is the creation of a systematic approach to redefining the Institute in a national and regional context, from public relations to professional education to audit practice. In January 2004, three years after her initiative, the relevant bill updating the Public Accountancy Act was passed in the Senate.

Under her stewardship, increased benefits were also provided for students, namely the staging of the first two joint ICAJ/ACCA graduation ceremonies, an extended study area for students, and an online website. She chaired the Public Relations and Publications Committee (ICAJ) 1993 to 1995 and 1997 to 1999, and she as a member of the ICAJ/IDB Steering Committee, the Audit Practice Committee and the Student Affairs Committee. She chaired the Organizing Committee for the 2003 Caribbean Conference of Accountants hosted by Jamaica.

A practising Fellow of the ICAJ and a Fellow of the Association of Chartered Certified Accountants (ACCA – United Kingdom), Hayle has also served on the boards of the Bank of Jamaica and the Institute of Chartered Accountants of the Caribbean. She represented the Caribbean and the Americas on the ACCA International Assembly for three consecutive two-year terms between 1998 and 2004.

In November 2001, the Board of the International Federation of Accountants (IFAC) appointed Hayle to its Compliance Committee for the 2001 to 2003 period. The Compliance Committee was responsible for the monitoring, support and regulatory process in relation to member body compliance with the rules and obligations of membership of IFAC.

As a sole practitioner, Carolyn Hayle operates as CPH Consulting, offering a range of accounting, audit and consulting services to businesses. She received the Distinguished Members Award in 2018.

21. L. Garth Kiddoe, FCA, MSc (Accounting) (2001–3)

First elected to Council in 1996, Garth Kiddoe served on the following committees: Continuing Professional Education (chairman), Taxation, Future of the Profession, Public Relations and Publications. He was vice-chairman of the PAB and member of the PSOJ Council. Kiddoe served as president of ICAC, 2006–7. He served as dean of the Faculty of Business and Management at the University of Technology, Jamaica.

22. Linroy Marshall, FCA, MSc, BSc (Mngmt), 2003–5

Marshall is a partner at KPMG. Prior to his appointment to the Council in 1998–99, he had served KPMG for nineteen years in Buffalo, New York, and in Kingston. He chaired the Audit Practice Committee of the ICAJ for sixteen years. He served as a member of the Investigations Committee of the ICAJ.

23. Leighton McKnight, OD, FCA, FCCA, BSc (2005–7)

An audit partner in the firm of PricewaterhouseCoopers, Leighton McKnight has responsibility for staff recruitment. He has over twenty years' experience in auditing, accounting and financial consulting, managing numerous technical financial engagements such as statutory financial audits, management audits and special financial and compliance audits in a wide range of industries.

McKnight was first elected to the Council of the ICAJ in 1997. He served as vice-president of the Institute in 2003 and 2004. He has chaired the Institute's Audit Practice Committee and also served as a member of the By-Laws, Finance, Admission, Student Affairs and Future of the Profession Committees.

McKnight has held leadership positions in a number of organizations and has served as chairman of the Government of Jamaica's Audit Commission and as a member of the Management Advisory Board of the Office of the Registrar of Companies. He has also served on the boards of entities including: Mutual Life Assurance Company, Jamaica Property Company Limited, the Scientific Research Council, the Football Foundation of Jamaica, Cornwall Old Boys Association and the UWI Guild of Graduates and on the committee of Jamaica's Parliamentary Integrity Commission

He is a distinguished past president of the Kiwanis Club of North St Andrew and is the certified Circle K Trainer for Eastern Canada & Caribbean District of Kiwanis International.

He has acted as visiting lecturer in auditing at the UWI, Mona, and a member of its mentorship programme. An active member of the Kingston Cricket and Pelicans Football Clubs, he enjoys outdoor sports, listening to music and reading.

He was appointed as Jamaica's representative to the ACCA International Assembly starting in 2009.

McKnight, also well known for his personal philanthropic pursuits, received ICAJ's Distinguished Member Award in 2017.

24. Prunella Vassell, FCA, FCCA (2007–9)

A graduate of CAST's School of Business, Prunella Vassell served as an associate of Paul Goldson in charge of audit services and tax consultancy. She joined the ICAJ Council in 1997. She has lectured at UTech, IMP and the Student's Consortium. Vassell served on the University Council of Jamaica's Advisory Board of the UTECH School of Business. She was vice-president, 2005–7 and president 2007–9. She has served on the Taxation, Admissions, Current Affairs, Public Relations, Future of the Profession Committees and has chaired the Student Affairs Committee. In 2003, she received the ICAJ's inaugural President's Award for Most Outstanding Chairperson in recognition of her contribution to the development of the Institute in her capacities as treasurer and chairman of the Public Relations and Publications Committee. An associate in charge of audit services and tax consultancy at UHY Dawgen, she has extensive experience in areas of Income Tax and GCT and lectured in accounting and taxation for many years. She has chaired the Management Committee of the Students' Accountancy Training Consortium, as well as its Technical Committee. She was a member of the Business Board of Studies of the UCJ, the Supervisory Board of the School of Business of UTech and the National Council on Education. Vassell was also Jamaica's representative to the ACCA International Assembly and director and treasurer of ICAC (2009).

25. Archibald Campbell, MSc, FCA (2009–11)

Archibald Campbell joined the Institute in 1984, was first elected to Council in 2002, was vice-president in 2007–9, and elected president in 2009. He served as chairman of the Taxation Committee and treasurer from 2005 to 2007. He also served as a member of the ICAJ's Accounting Standards, Continuing Professional Development (CPD), Current Affairs, Future of the Profession and Membership Committees. A graduate of CAST and UWI, he worked in auditing at Touche Ross Thorburn (now Deloitte), and has worked in commercial and merchant banking, as well as in the insurance industry.

He was a lecturer in the Department of Management Studies, UWI, Mona, where he taught financial statement analysis, risk and treasury management and advanced financial accounting. He is co-editor of "An Ethical Perspective of Caribbean Businesses" and the co-author of two academic papers on the financial sector crisis of 1997.

In addition to these accomplishments, he has served as an accounting expert in settling a commercial dispute involving an international company and has served as an expert accounting witness.

He is a regular trainer on corporate governance to the Private Sector Organization of Jamaica, Jamaica's Ministry of Finance, and the Eastern Caribbean Stock Exchange. He also serves as a presenter for numerous technical seminars hosted by the ICAJ.

Campbell has served as the deputy chairman of the Board of Directors of Jamaica Money Market Brokers Limited, as director of JMMB Securities Limited, and chairman of the company's Audit Committee. He was a member of the Government of Jamaica's Sugar Negotiating Team, which had responsibility for the divestment of the sugar industry.

He has also been a member of the boards of directors of various corporate entities, including Mutual Security Bank (Cayman) Limited, which was his brainchild, NCB Cayman Ltd, International Hotels Ltd (Hedonism II),

Edward Gayle & Company, NCB Investments Ltd and Jamaica Mutual Property Company Limited. He is a member and past director of the Kiwanis Club of North St Andrew.

26. Vintoria Bernard, FCA, FCCA (2011–13)

A Clarendon College graduate, Bernard has been in practice since 1991 as a sole practitioner – the managing partner of VB Chartered Accountants – following an eight-year stint at PricewaterhouseCoopers. A member of the ICAJ since 1987, she was elected to the ICAJ's Council in 2005. She chaired the Public Relations and Publications, and Taxation Committees and joined the Institute's Continuing Professional Development Committee in 1997. Vice-president in 2009–11, Bernard was elected president of the ICAJ in 2011, the third female to serve in that capacity. She has served as Jamaica's representative to the ACCA International Assembly. Bernard is a Fellow of the Institute, as well as a Fellow of the Association of Chartered Certified Accountants (ACCA). She also provided invaluable support in the organization of the Institute of Chartered Accountants of the Caribbean (ICAC), serving as director and treasurer as well as on several ICAC Conference committees.

She has a wealth of experience in general management, as well as internal and external auditing, some of which was acquired during her employment at PricewaterhouseCoopers. Her range of skills was widened by corporate stints in statutory organizations and the manufacturing and distribution sectors. She has been a member of the Board of JMMB Merchant Bank.

Bernard was the leader-founder of the fifth all-female Kiwanis Club (Eastern St Andrew), which was chartered in 1995. It is a tribute to her leadership skills and commitment that the Eastern St Andrew Club was the only local club to become "Distinguished" within the first year of its charter.

27. Dennis Chung, FCA, MSc, CPA (California) (2013–15)

A Jamaica College old boy, Dennis Chung completed his BSc and MSc (Accounting) in 1987 and 1989, respectively, at the UWI. He also has a CPA from California. Admitted to the ICAJ Council in 2005, he became vice-president in 2011 and was elected president in 2013. He has also served as chairman of ICAJ's Membership, Continuing Professional Development and Property Development Committees.

Chung was appointed chief executive officer of the Private Sector Organisation of Jamaica (PSOJ) on 1 May 2013. A former director at the Bank of Jamaica, Statistical Institute of Jamaica, Jamaica Urban Transit Company, the Betting, Gaming and Lotteries Commission, and the Kiwanis Club of North St Andrew, he was also a member of the National Services Task Force as a part of Jamaica's Vision 2030 Plan. In 2017 he was appointed chief financial officer of Supreme Ventures Group (as of February 2018). In 2017 he was chairman of the National Solid Waste Management Authority, National Integrity Action and the Pension Fund Association of Jamaica. He is the author of *Charting Jamaica's Economic and Social Development: A Much Needed Paradigm Shift*, which examines Jamaica's macroeconomic numbers since the 1960s and suggests a way forward for economic and social development.

He has been a member of the Jamaica College Board and Foundation since 2005.

28. Bruce Scott, FCA, FCCA, CISA, MBA (Manchester Business School), CPA (Colorado) (2015–17)

Bruce Scott received his primary education at Holy Family Primary School and his secondary education at Jamaica College. As a student at Jamaica College, he discovered his "insatiable" desire to be a chartered accountant. Immediately following his 'A' Levels at Jamaica College, he took up employment at PricewaterhouseCoopers (PwC), which played a major role in creating the right environment for him to study. While there he completed all three levels of the ACCA in record time, in 1993, by age twenty-one. Taariq Abdul Majeed, and then twenty-year old Paul Hyman have subsequently broken the record. As a partner at PwC, he has responsibility for the Risk Assurance practices in Jamaica and the network of PwC firms in the Caribbean (onshore territories). As a member of ICAJ's Council, he served as chairman of the Membership, Student Affairs, Property Development and the Public Relations and Publications Committees. Scott also chaired a Funding Committee (which had a specific mandate and term) that made recommendations on how the activities of the Institute could be funded as part of a broader goal to ensure the future sustainability of the Institute. Scott also served as a member of the Student Society Executive in his days as a student. He served as alternate director on the ICAC Board. Scott served as technical advisor to Pamela Monroe-Ellis in her capacity as a board member of the International Federation of Accountants – the first representatives from the Caribbean to do so. His Christian beliefs, which mean a lot to him, are encapsulated in his words: "I am a Christian who happens to be an accountant."

29. Raymond Campbell, JP, FCA, FCCA, CBV, BSc (Accounting), UWI (elected 2017)

Raymond Campbell is a partner at KPMG, which he joined in 2006 as a principal in the advisory services practice in Jamaica. Raymond Campbell has over twenty-eight years' experience in the financial and professional services sector, and for the last twenty-five years held managerial positions in the securities and banking industries. His professional skills are in the areas of M&A deal structuring, valuations, loan structuring, deal negotiations, strategic planning, business analysis, securities and banking operations and financing strategies.

A member of ICAJ since 2010 and Council member since 2011, Campbell has served in several capacities including chairman of the Institute of Chartered Accountants of the Caribbean (ICAC) 2011 Conference in Jamaica and chairman of the ICAJ's Public Relations, Future of the Profession and Property Development Committees.

He formerly served as the executive director, Capital Markets for First Caribbean International Bank and Country Manager at CIBC Jamaica Limited (First Caribbean International Bank, Jamaica) where, as the bank's principal officer in Jamaica, he developed excellent relationships with local and regional regulators, as well as government ministries and agencies. Within the bank, he served on the regional Executive Management Committee and was a member of the bank's Integration Steering Committee.

Throughout his work life, he has gained various professional qualifications including Fellow of the Association of Chartered Certified Accountants in 1998, membership of the Canadian Institute of Chartered Business Valuators in 2010 and the Canadian Securities Course in 1991.

In 2016, he became a justice of the peace for St Andrew. He is a council member at the Bethel Baptist Church in Half-Way-Tree, and currently serves as vice-president of the Constant Spring Golf Club. Campbell has also served as president of the Jamaica Bankers' Association and chairman of the Jamaica Institute of Bankers.

He is a regular conference speaker. In his spare time, he likes to play golf and spend time with family and friends.

Appendix 2

First Members of ICAJ

1. J. D. Ashenheim
2. O. T. Brown
3. S. N. Bryan
4. D. P. Goldson
5. Paul Goldson
6. Peter Harty
7. R. C. Harty
8. Edgar C. Jones
9. James F. L. Lord
10. A. R. McClure
11. Gerald Mair
12. A. R. Marsh
13. C. V. Kay
14. J. W. Riley
15. E. Clinton Nunes
16. Philmore Ogle
17. Peter Puddle
18. E. Caroll Thorburn
19. William A. Thwaites
20. R. Williams

Appendix 3

ICAJ Golden Jubilee Song (Original)

The dreams of our founding fathers are now bearing fruit
Proud and strong this is where we belong
Through strife and hardship we never sway
Institute of Chartered Accountants of Jamaica
We are the ICAJ.

Chorus

ICAJ – Keep the dream alive
ICAJ – Together we survive
ICAJ – Golden Jubilee
ICAJ – Vere et digne

Reference point for Chartered Accountants
Producing nation builders, leaders in our community
Financial professionals, business advisors
Members, associates, affiliates
Let's keep the dream alive.

Chorus

Fifty years of stellar service
Golden association with each practice
Building on our gains
Charting our future
With one accord we must say
In God we trust to lead the way.

Notes

Chapter 1

1. Francisco Morales Padrón, *Spanish Jamaica* (Kingston: Ian Randle, 2003), 124.
2. B.W. Higman, *Slave Population and Economy in Jamaica, 1807–1834* (Cambridge: Cambridge University Press, 1976), 9–10.
3. B.W. Higman, *Plantation Jamaica, 1759–1950: Capital and Control in a Colonial Economy* (Kingston: University of the West Indies Press, 2005), 101.
4. Ibid., 96.
5. Ibid., 101.
6. David Gosse, *Abolition and Plantation Management in Jamaica, 1802–1838* (Kingston: University of the West Indies Press, 2003), 46.
7. Ibid., 48.
8. Patrick Bryan, *The Jamaican People, 1880–1902: Race, Class and Social Control* (Kingston: University of the West Indies Press, 2000), 142.
9. Ken Shackleton and Stephen Walker, *Professional Reconstruction: The Coordination of the Accountancy Bodies, 1930–1957* (Institute of Chartered Accountants of Scotland, 1998), executive summary, v, https://www.icas.com/_data/assetspdffile/0018/10557/94-Professional-Reconstruction-icas.pdf.
10. Marcia Annisette, "Imperialism and the Professions: The Education and Certification of Accountants in Trinidad and Tobago", *Accounting, Organizations and Society* 25 (2000), 638.
11. Ibid., 640.
12. Ibid., 639.
13. Bryan, *Jamaican People*, 26.
14. "Profile Deloite and Touche: Chartered Accountants, 1949–1999", *ICAJ Newsletter* (April 1999), henceforth *ICAJ-N*.
15. T. Cristina Maria, "The Impact of the Great Depression on American Accountancy Practice", *Annals of Faculty of Economics* 1, no. 2 (December 2012): 727.

16. Geoffrey W. Smith, "Data Processing. A Challenge to the Accounting Profession", Annual Convention of the Institute of Chartered Accountants of Jamaica, 8–9 October 1976, ICAJ Archives, Ogle Papers, File Index 15.
17. Shackleton and Walker, *Professional Reconstruction*, 71.
18. Ibid.
19. "The Future Organisation of the Accountancy Profession", *ICAJ-N* 4, no. 1 (November 1994): 1.
20. Shackleton and Walker, *Professional Reconstruction*, ix.
21. Ibid., 96.
22. Paris Dubravka, "History and Accounting", *Journal of Accounting and Management* 6, no. 1 (2016): 1.
23. W. Adolphe Roberts, *These Many Years: An Autobiography*, ed. Peter Hulme (Kingston: University of the West Indies Press, 2015).
24. Gladstone Mills, *Grist for the Mills: Reflections on a Life* (Kingston: Ian Randle, 1994), 99.
25. "Uriel Salmon: A Man for all Seasons", *Charter* (Summer 1997): 15–19.
26. Author's interview with Jasper Burnett, 23 February 2017.
27. Burnett to W.H. Kruger, 2 February 1979. Working Papers and Minutes of Council ICAJ, 9 June 1977 to 24 May 1979.
28. Carroll Thorburn, "My Early Years in Auditing, 1946–47", *Charter* (Spring 2000).
29. *Jamaica Observer*, 23 December 2013.
30. Mills, *Grist for the Mills*, 54.
31. Marcia Annisette, "Imperialism and the Professions", 653.
32. O. Bakre, "Imperialism and Professionalization: The Case of Accountancy in Jamaica" in *Accountancy and Empire*. The British Legacy of Professional Organization eds. Chris Pouillas and Suki Sian (London: Routledge, 2010).
33. Alfred Rattray quoted in Margaret Mendes and Rachael McLean, *Regulatory Framework of Accounting in Jamaica* (Kingston: CFM, 1982) (third edition 2001), 389.
34. Annisette, "Imperialism and the Professions", 650.
35. Owolabe Bakre, "The First Attempt at Localising Imperial Accountancy. The Case of the Institute of Chartered Accountants of Jamaica (ICAJ) 1950s–1970s", *Critical Perspectives in Accounting 16*, 995–1018.

Chapter 2

1. "Profile of Philmore Ogle", *Charter* (Summer 1996), 13. In his account of the formation of the Institute ("Advent of the Institute"), Philmore Ogle mentions the role of Alfred Rattray from the public sector, Vernon Chang-Alloy, Horace Hardy-Henry, Linton Minott, Denis Goldson and James Lord. "The Young Turks", Ogle emphasizes, "longed for Jamaica to be independent with its own institutions, and they felt impelled to be involved in new-nation building."
2. Correspondence between author and Philmore Ogle, 30 January 2018. See also Jamaica Debates Commission. "Commissioner, Philmore Ogle", 28 December 2016.
3. *Council Minutes* (henceforth CM), 1973.
4. Jasper Burnett, "The ICAJ- Origins and Focus", in *The Institute of Chartered Accountants of Jamaica: The First Twenty- Five Years, 1965–1990,* ed. Jasper Burnett (Kingston: Institute of Chartered Accountants of Jamaica, 1990), 16.
5. Bakre, "First Attempt", 1017.
6. Robert Lightbourne, *Daily Gleaner*, 27 November 1968.
7. Ibid.
8. Author's interview with Philmore Ogle.
9. "Profile on Philmore Ogle, a Founding Member of the ICAJ", *Charter* (1996): 13.
10. Public Accountancy Act, paragraphs 18 and 21.
11. Ibid., 25.
12. Alastair MacBeath, "Report to Council", CM, 21 December 1975.
13. Ibid.
14. Author's correspondence with Philmore Ogle, 30 January 2018, enclosing dates of correspondence between the Institute and the ACCA.
15. Annual Report (henceforth AR) 1984–85, Kenneth Lewis, "President's Statement", 1.
16. *Charter* (Summer 1987), 9, and author's interview with Elizabeth Hartley, 21 February 2017. CACA or the Chartered Association of Certified Accountants refers to the ACCA.
17. C.P. Cacho, "The Accountancy Profession in the Commonwealth Caribbean" (unpublished paper, 1968), 5
18. Marcia Annisette, "Imperialism and the Profession. The Education and Certification of Accountants in Trinidad and Tobago", 639.
19. Philmore Ogle, "Advent of the Institute" (unpublished paper, 2 July 2015, Ogle Papers) and author's interview with Ogle, 12 April 2017. In 1965 the acronym ACCA stood for Association of Certified and Corporate Accountants". See Institute of Chartered Accountants of Jamaica, "The Matter of Examinations: Significant Dates", 28 November 1964.
20. Institute of Chartered Accountants of Jamaica, "The Matter of Exams".

21. Jamaica Archives, "Proposed Amendments to the Revised Draft of the Agreement Establishing the Caribbean Examinations Council", Enclosure to Cabinet Submission "The Establishment of a Caribbean Examinations Council", quoted in Patrick E. Bryan, *A History of the Caribbean Examinations Council, 1973–2013* (Barbados: Caribbean Examinations Council, 2015), 20.
22. CM, 5 November 1999, "By-Law Changes".
23. "ICAJ Vice-President (Mrs C. Patricia Hayle) to Serve on the International Assembly Representing the Caribbean and the Americas", *ICAJ-N* (June 1998): 8.
24. AR 1978–79, "Acknowledgements", 5.
25. Ibid., AR 2000–2001, "Awards 2000", 14.
26. Burnett, "Training of Accountants: A Discussion Paper Between the Public Accountancy Board and the Council of the Institute of Chartered Accountants of Jamaica", 18 May 1982.
27. Ibid.
28. AR 2015–16, "Notes to Financial Statements", 59.
29. AR 2015–16, "Related Party Transactions", 71.
30. Press release, 16 December 1975.
31. Jasper Burnett, "The Future of the Accountancy Profession in Jamaica", 18 April 1978.
32. *Charter*, no.2 (May 1980): 1.
33. Address of Phillip Aspinall, President of ICA of Quebec, at Annual ICAJ Dinner, 2 December 1977 and published in the *Daily Gleaner*, 6 December 1977.
34. ICAJ Bulletin "What Is an Accountant?"
35. Mills, *Grist for the Mills*, 55.
36. "Report to Council", CM September 2006.
37. AR 1997–98, "Geographical Distribution of Members".

Chapter 3

1. Dereck Sale, "The Institute of Chartered Accountants of Jamaica: Thinking about Tomorrow" in Burnett, *Institute of Chartered Accountants*, 147–50.
2. Carroll Thorburn, "Role of Practising Accountants in Jamaica Today", in Burnett, *Institute of Chartered Accountants*, 42–45.
3. Burnett, "Talk Given to the Quarterly Luncheon of the ICAJ by the President of the Institute", 15 February 1978.
4. *Sunday Gleaner*, 18 April 1976, "Professional Advisory Services".
5. Alastair MacBeath, "Review of Published Accounts", *Charter* 1 no. 2 (May 1980): 19.
6. Message from ICAJ President, Vintoria Bernard 2011.

7. Press Release, "Dereck Sale Heads Chartered Accountants", *Jamaica Daily News*, Sunday 25 July 1976.
8. Author's interview with Philmore Ogle, 2 March 2017.
9. CM, 13 January 1977.
10. Ibid.
11. *Daily Gleaner*, 15 April 1979.
12. CM, 11 August 1977.
13. "Where are They Now?" *Charter* 1 no. 2 (May 1980): 32.
14. Chartered Accountants Press Release, "President of Chartered Accountants of Jamaica Speaks to American Businessmen in West Palm Beach, Florida, November 15, 1976."
15. AR 1980–1, "President's Statement", 1.
16. Edward Seaga, *Edward Seaga: My Life and Leadership*, vol. 2: *Hard Road to Travel 1980–2008* (Oxford: Macmillan, 2010), 56 and 58–59.
17. Ibid., 57.
18. *Daily Gleaner*, 22 December 2011.
19. Seaga, *My Life and Leadership* (vol. 2), 56.
20. AR 1983–4, "President's Statement", 2.
21. AR 1985–6, "President Madden's Statement", 3. See also Aulous Madden, "Address to the PSOJ, 13 March 1987 in "Reflections: My Term in Office". See also "Statement on the Report of the Tax Reform Committee (1985). Address to the Annual Christmas Luncheon of the Institute of Chartered Accountants of Jamaica by its President, Aulous Madden, 4th December, 1985." Aulous Madden, "Reflections: My Term in Office" (Vol. 1) and Aulous Madden, President's Remarks to New Members' [PSOJ] Reception", 28 November 1986.
22. Seaga, *My Life and Leadership*, 2:87.
23. AR 1986–87, "Taxation Committee", 14.
24. Jasper Burnett, "Training of Accountants", 19 May 1982.
25. Roy Bahl, "The Jamaican Tax Reform: The Design and Performance", in *Tax Reform in Developing Countries*, ed. Wayne Thirsk (Washington, DC: World Bank, 1987), chapter 5, 167–231.
26. "News Stand" *Charter* 4 (May 1981), 7.
27. Dennis Brown, "'Migration' to International Accounting Standards", *ICAJ-N* (May 2001): 2.
28. "IASC" *Charter* (May 1981): 9.
29. AR 1978–79, "Legal Matters", 4.
30. CM 9 March 1977, 11 February 1979 and 26 February 1979.
31. CM 26 February 1979, and *Gleaner*, 11 February 1979.
32. J.J. Jolly to editor, *Daily Gleaner*, 8 December 1975.
33. M.J. Mepham, "The Accountancy Profession in Jamaica", in *Twenty-Five Years*, 47.

34. Burnett, "Training of Accountants".
35. Philmore Ogle, draft response, ICAJ Archives, Ogle Papers, File Index 15.
36. Ogle to President Alastair MacBeath, 16 October 1974.
37. CM 12 October 1978.
38. "Profile of Kenneth La Cruise", in *Charter* (Spring 2000): 15. Also Jasper Burnett, interview with the author.
39. CM 10 April 1980.
40. CM 6 March 1980.
41. CM 9 April 1980.
42. CM 26 February 1982.
43. CM memo of Jasper Burnett 17 June 1980.

Chapter 4

1. CM AGM 19 June 1973.
2. CM 14 November 1968, "Report of Future of the Profession Committee to Council", tabled 12 October 1968.
3. ICAJ Archives, Ogle Papers, press release, 25 June 1970.
4. Probably because of the economic situation in Jamaica in the late 1970s, the basis of funding for the CAST programme (subscriptions from accounting firms) ended in 1977.
5. Minister of Marketing and Commerce, enclosure to CM, 23 September 1976.
6. Ibid.
7. "Speech by Minister of Industry and Commerce", 2 December 1977, ICAJ Archives, Burnett Working Papers.
8. Ibid.
9. Meeting of PAB, ICAJ, and Minister of Industry, 13 November 1978. On 21 May 1979 Burnett received word from the government (S.T. Graham to Burnett) that financial help would not be forthcoming for the training of accountants, since the government was concentrating on "matters of high national priority".
10. D.C. Sale, 11 May 1976.
11. Notes of minister's meeting with ICAJ and PAB, 13 November 1978.
12. See chapter 7.
13. Correspondence between Principal of CAST, Alfred Sangster, Paul Saulter and Jasper Burnett, 6 October 1978, 8 November 1978, and 25 November 1979.
14. CM 9 March 1978.
15. Speech by minister of industry and commerce, 2 December 1977.

16. Carl W. Gray, Chairman Students' Committee, Memorandum to ICAJ, "Developments at CAST and Their Impact on the Future Training of Accountants", 19 January 1978.
17. AR 1978–79, "Education: UWI & CAST", 3.
18. AR 1979–80, "Future of the Profession", 15.
19. Randolph Williams, "UWI and the Caribbean Accounting Profession", *ICAJ-N* (March 1993): 3.
20. Burnett, "Future of the Accounting Profession in Jamaica", 18 April 1978.
21. Aulous Madden, "The MSc Accounting Programme – Whither?" *Charter* (October-December 2000): 22.
22. A.Z. Preston, having served as bursar and pro-vice-chancellor (finance) at UWI, served as vice-chancellor of that institution from 1974 to 1986. He was also chairman of the PAB.
23. "ICAJ Press Release", *Daily News*, Sunday, 25 July 1975, 6.
24. A.Z. Preston, "Address at the 21st Anniversary Banquet of the ICAJ held at the Jamaica Pegasus on Saturday September 21, 1985", 10.
25. Ibid., 9–10.
26. Alister McIntyre, *The Caribbean and the Wider World: Commentaries on My Life and Career* (Kingston: University of the West Indies Press, 2016), 214.
27. Margaret Mendes, "Innovation in Professional Accountancy Education at the University of the West Indies (Jamaica): 1968–88" (MA thesis, UWI, 1990), 174.
28. Burnett, "Future of Accountancy Profession".
29. "Chartered Accountants 1944–1999", *ICAJ-N* (April 1999): 2.
30. Dereck Sale to A.Z. Preston, CM 1977–78, 30 May 1977.
31. A.Z. Preston to Brian Mair, 25 June 1977, CM 1977–78.
32. AR 1979–80, "Educational Trust", 15.
33. 1979–80, "Director of Studies", 15; and Jasper Burnett, "Report on Behalf of Future of Accounting Profession in Jamaica", 18 April 1978.
34. CM, Annual General Meeting, 16 June 1976.
35. Aulous Madden, "The UWI MSc", *Charter* (October–December 1990): 22.
36. Mendes, "Innovation in Professional Accountancy", 186.
37. "William Thwaites Interview with John Jackson in Burnett, *Institute of Chartered Accountants*, 6.
38. Ibid.6
39. Bakre, "First Attempt, 905– 1019". See also O. Bakre, "The Second Attempt at Localising Imperial Accountancy: The Case of the Institute of Chartered Accountants of Jamaica (ICAJ)", *Critical Perspectives in Accountancy* 17, no. 1 (2006): 1–28.
40. Mendes, "Innovation in Professional Accountancy", 178–82.
41. Ibid., 172.

42. Burnett, "Discussion Paper", 1982, 2.
43. Mendes, "An Examination of Jamaica's Accountancy Training Problems and the Development of a Three Tiered Training Model as a Possible Solution. Part 1: An Examination of Jamaica's Accountancy Training Problems" (unpublished paper, 1983), 45–46.
44. Ibid., 32.
45. AR 1991, "MSc Accounting Degree", 15.
46. Author's Interview with Prunella Vassell and C. Patricia Hayle, 16 November 2017.
47. O. Bakre, "Imperialism and Professionalisation: The Case of Accountancy in Jamaica", chapter 7, 144–67 in Poullaos and Suki Sian, *Accountancy and Empire.*

Chapter 5

1. Carroll Thorburn to Jasper Burnett, 1 April 1981, ICAJ Archives, Burnett Working Papers.
2. "Interview with President of IFAC", *Charter* (May 1981), 17.
3. Keith Mitchell, prime minister of Grenada, at the Ninth International Meeting, St George's Grenada, 2 March 1998, in *Integrate or Perish! Perspectives of Leaders of the Integration Movement, 1963–1999,* ed. Kenneth Hall (Kingston: University of the West Indies, CARICOM Institutional Project Mona, 2000), 561. P.J. Patterson, "18th Meeting of the Conference of Heads of Government of the Caribbean Community", Montego Bay June 4–July 1997, in ibid., 47–53.
4. Dennis Irvine, "Information on the Caribbean Examinations Council", *Information on the Caribbean Examinations Council,* vol. 2 (Kingston: Western Zone Office, 25 July 1978), 3.
5. B.T.I. Pollard, "Status of Company Law in the Region and the Need for Company Law Reform", *ICAJ-N* (September 1987): 3.
6. "ICAJ Gets Research Grant for Company Law Reform", *ICAJ-N* (September 1987): 1; and AR 1987–88, "Company Law Reform Committee", 8.
7. AGM 16 June 1976.
8. AR 1993–94, 12; AR 1994–95, "Finance", 12.
9. Aulous Madden, interview by the author, 16 January 2018.
10. P.J. Patterson, deputy prime minister of Jamaica, "Challenges and Opportunities in the 1990s", in *First Twenty-Five Years,* 161.
11. Selby Wilson, "The Caribbean Accountants: Towards Integration", in *First Twenty-Five Years,* 156.
12. Aulous Madden, "What Will the ICAC Mean?", in *First Twenty-Five Years,* 155.
13. *ICAJ-N* (December 1988): 4.

14. Madden, "What Will the ICAC Mean?", 155.
15. AR October 2006, "President's Report", and Interview with Prunella Vassell and Patricia Hayle.
16. ICAC, *Links Newsletter* (January –April 2017), 19.
17. ICAC, Annual Report (1997), 14.
18. CM 4 May 2000.
19. AR 1987–88, "Institute of Chartered Accountants of the Caribbean", 9.
20. Linroy Marshall, "The Future of Our Profession", *ICAJ-N* (July 2001): 6.
21. Author's Interviews with Archibald Campbell and Vintoria Bernard.
22. Keith Mitchell, "Ninth Inter-Sessional Meeting", in Kenneth O. Hall, *Integrate or Perish: Perspectives of Leaders of the Integration Movement, 1963–1999* (Kingston: University of the West Indies/CARICOM Project, 2000), 560–61.
23. Ian Boxill, *Ideology and Caribbean Integration* (Kingston: Consortium Graduate School of Social Sciences, UWI, Mona, 1993), 61.
24. CM, 13 November 2008.
25. AR 1986–7, "MSc Accounting Programme Committee", 12.
26. O. Bakre, "Integration and Conflict of Identity: An Analysis of the Development of the Accountancy Profession in the Commonwealth Caribbean" (Madrid, Spain, 13–16 July 2003), 19.
27. Randolph Williams, "UWI and the Caribbean Accounting Profession", *ICAJ-N* (March 1993).
28. PAB Minutes, 19 February 1991.
29. See previous chapter re UWI/ICAJ impasse.
30. O.M. Bakre, "Integration and Conflict of Identity", 19.
31. Author's interview with Vintoria Bernard, 17 November 2017.
32. Author's interview with Bruce Scott.
33. C. Patricia Hayle, "Future of the Profession Committee", 20 June 2000.
34. "MSc Renewed", *ICAJ-N* (May 1997): 3.
35. Author's interviews with Archibald Campbell (21 November 2017) and Bruce Scott (29 November 2017); and AR 2005–6, "Regional Collaboration", 10.

Chapter 6

1. AR 2001, "Library: Performance Highlights", 13.
2. ICAJ Supplement, *Daily Gleaner*, Message from ICAJ President, Vintoria Bernard.
3. Winston Dookeran, "Excerpts from keynote address delivered by Winston Dookeran, Governor of the Central Bank of Trinidad and Tobago, at the Opening of the 18th Annual Caribbean Conference of Accountants", *ICAJ-N* (July 2000): 5.

4. J.A. Burggraaff, "The Need for Standards and the Role of Standard Setting Agencies", *Charter* (May 1981): 11.
5. John Waite, "Reflections of an Expatriate Accountant", *Charter* 1 no. 2 (May 1980): 14.
6. "International Standards of Accounting and Reporting", in ibid., 30.
7. "Members shall ensure that measures not subject to scheduling under Articles XVI or XVII of the GATS, relating to licensing requirements and procedures, technical standards and qualification requirements and procedures are not prepared, adopted or applied with a view to or with the effect of creating unnecessary barriers to trade in accountancy services." https://www-wto.org.
8. Patricia Arnold, "Disciplining Domestic Regulation: The World Trade Organization and the Market for Professional Services", *Accounting, Organizations and Society* 30 (2005): 305.
9. Ibid. 307.
10. "IFAC Applauds World Trade Organisation", *ICAJ-N* (30 September 1997): 7.
11. Arnold, "Disciplining", 315.
12. AR 2002–3, "Report of President Garth Kiddoe", 6.
13. CM, 4 March 1998.
14. Everton McDonald, "Deregulation and the Profession", *Charter* (October–December 1990): 1.
15. "Uriel Salmon: A Man for All Seasons", *Charter* (Summer 1997): 19.
16. Omar Davies, speech given at the Twenty-First Conference of ICAC, 27 June 2003, Ritz Carlton, Jamaica (ICAJ File: Speeches), 4.
17. "Accountants Challenged to Observe Code of Ethics", *ICAJ-N* (October 1999): 1.
18. https://en.wikipedia.org/wiki/Causes_of_the_Great_Recession (retrieved: 19 June 2017). See also AR 2003–4, "President's Report" (Linroy Marshall), 8.
19. AR 1997–98, "President's Report", 6.
20. "Concerned Practitioner", letter to the editor, *ICAJ-N* (July 2001): 6.
21. Interviews with immediate past presidents, Bruce Scott and C. Patricia Hayle.
22. Davies, speech, 27 June 2003.
23. Ibid., 7.
24. *ICAJ-N*, President's Message (May 1997): 6; President's Message *ICAJ-N* (September 1997): 1.
25. "Can Auditors Be Jailed for Not Reporting?" *ICAJ-N* (December 1997): 1. See AR 2007–8, 17, and Banking Act 1997: 42 (3). "Where any person commits an offence against this Act or any regulations hereunder for which no penalty is expressly provided shall be liable to a fine not exceeding $500,000 or imprisonment for a term not exceeding six months."
26. AR 2007–8, "Audit Practice Committee: Legislative Options to Protect Auditors from Catastrophic Lawsuits", 17.

27. Davies, speech, 6 and 9.
28. AR 2000–2001, "President's Report", 6.
29. Ibid.
30. AR 2003–4, "President's Report".
31. "There is," declared Aston Preston in 1985, "after all a tradition of abuse alongside the distinguished track record of the profession over the last century" (A.Z. Preston, address at the Twenty-First Anniversary Banquet of the ICAJ held at the Pegasus on Saturday, 21 September 1986). Recognizing that morality and law are not coterminous, the minister of finance admitted that "one will never be able to eliminate all malpractices" (Davies, speech, 4).
32. CM, 13 July 2000, Section K, Review of Code of Ethics.
33. IFAC Code of Ethics for Professional Accountants Section 100.1, https//:www.ifac.org/system/files/publications/files/ifac_code_of_ethics_for.pdf.
34. AR 2001–2, "Audit Practice: Code of Ethics", 11.
35. Dennis Brown, "Migration to International Accounting Standards", *ICAJ-N* (May 2001): 2.
36. AR 2000–2001, "Accounting Standards: Performance Highlights", 9.
37. AR 2012–13, "Notes to Financial Statements", 53n14.
38. Author's interview with Vintoria Bernard.
39. AR 2005–6, "Report of President Leighton McKnight", 7.
40. CM, 11 February 2008.
41. AR 1978–9, "President's Statement", 1.
42. AR 1977–78, "Continuing Education", 11.
43. By-Law 33 (1) (a).
44. AR 2004–5, "Resolutions", 5.
45. AR 1999–2000, "Continuing Professional Education Committee".
46. Henri Fortin, Ana Cristina Barros and Kit Cutler, *Accounting for Growth in Latin America and the Caribbean. Improving Corporate Financial Reporting to Support Regional Economic Development* (Washington DC: World Bank, 2010), 51.
47. Jasper Burnett, "Report to Council", 18 April 1978.
48. "ICAJ Set to Become Sole Official Agents of PAB", *ICAJ-N* (May 2000): 1.
49. Executive Summary, "Legal and Administrative Framework for the Practice of Accountancy in Jamaica", 2000.
50. *ICAC-N*, May 2004, 4.
51. "ICAJ Set to become Sole Official Agents", *ICAJ-N* (May 2001): 1.
52. AR 2012–13, "Duplication of Functions by ICAJ and PAB", 17.
53. AR 2007–8, "Practice Monitoring Project for Practitioners", 8.
54. "Contract Schedule", ICAJ General Collection.
55. Davies, speech, 11.

56. Ministry Paper #56 September 2002; Steven Jackson, "Government Moves towards Eliminating Deferred Payment with Accrual Accounting", *Jamaica Observer*, 16 April 2014.
57. CM, 11 May 2006, "Report of Public Sector Committee".
58. AR 2011–12, "Public Sector Committee: IPSAS/Accrual Accounting", 20.
59. CM, 4 May 2000. ICAJ File: "Future of the Profession", 2000.
60. AR 2000–2001, "Public Sector Committee", 13.
61. AR 2015–16, "Report of President" (Bruce Scott), 7.
62. ICAJ Archives, Certified General Accountant Canada 2000; Report of Executive Director of ICAJ, 2006.
63. AR 2010–11, "CMA Canada" (Certified Management Accountant), 16.
64. AR 2004–5, "President's Report", 9.

Chapter 7

1. AR 2015–16, "Property, Plant and Equipment", 60. By 2015 the buildings were valued at $125,800,000 by independent chartered surveyors, "on a replacement cost basis, for insurance purposes".
2. They were required to have both mathematics and English (at O level). An A-level certificate was a plus. Recruits had to be over sixteen years of age.
3. AR 2015–16, "ACCA/ICAJ Student Recruitment Drive", 19.
4. CM, 11 August 1977.
5. Fortin, Barros, Cutler, *Accounting for Growth in Latin America and the Caribbean*, 70.
6. Mendes, "Innovation and Professional Accountancy", 175.
7. AR 1977–78, "Students", 15.
8. Jasper Burnett, 18 April 1978, "The ICAJ: Future of the Accountancy Profession in Jamaica".
9. AR 1998–99, Student Affairs, "Orientation/Rap Sessions", 11.
10. CM 14 February 2008, "Report of Student Affairs Committee".
11. AR 2010–11 "Promoting ICAJ", 21.
12. Author's interview with Philmore Ogle, 2 March 2017.
13. Students' Society, "Rules and Regulations", July 1977 and 22 March 1978.
14. Ibid.
15. CM, 9 March 1977.
16. Norman Creary, "Neglect of Jamaican Accounting Students", Letter to editor, *Daily Gleaner*, 20 June 1987. For the Consortium see 180 ff.
17. Aulous Madden, "Address to Students Accountancy Training Consortium. Motivational Meeting", 15 March 1986.
18. CM, October 1999, "Members' Survey Summarised Results", 5.

19. Teddy Charles, "Student Chairman Speaks of Institute" in *First Twenty-Five Years,* 214. Students committed to the Joint ICAJ/ACCA scheme paid $10.00 to the ICAJ and a £14 annual subscription to the ACCA in 1981. CM 26 February, 1981. Continued depreciation of the Jamaican currency would have led to increased student fees.
20. Concerned Students, "Some Major Sore Points" (open letter to Institute), Pre-Chartered, supplement to *ICAJ-N*, 1, no. 1 (November 1992).
21. AR 1997–98, "Future of the Profession", 12.
22. CM, 7 October 2000, "Internal Look/Analysis of the ICAJ".
23. AR 1997–98, "Future of the Profession", 12.
24. Annual General Meeting of Student Society, 26 March 1980.
25. "Students' Rap", *ICAJ-N* (December 1996): 5.
26. Annual General Meeting of Student Society, 26 March 1980; C*harte*r 1 no. 2 (May 1980): 28.
27. AR 1985–86, "Student Affairs", 9.
28. "Overall Award Winner – Dion Staple", *ICAJ-N* (December 1999): 5.
29. Ibid., 4.
30. AR 2012–13, Student Affairs Committee, "ICAJ/ACCA Joint Scheme Examinations", 21.
31. Elizabeth Hartley, "Report on the Future of the Students' Accountancy Training Consortium" (unpublished paper, n.d.).
32. AR 1994–95, "Student Affairs", 14.
33. AR 1987–88, "President's Statement", 4.
34. Rose Campbell-Patrick, "Consistency of Purpose is the Key to Success", *ICAJ-N* (November 1994): 4.
35. AR 1985–86, "Examinations", 9; AR 1986–87, "Student Affairs", 13; AR 1987–88, "Student Affairs", 12.
36. AR 1999–2000, "Student Affairs", 7.
37. Hartley, "Report on the Future of the Student Accountancy Training Consortium".
38. Ibid., also author's interviews with 2017 Hayle and Vassell (16 November 2017).
39. *Daily Gleaner*, 14 October 2017, "Too Many Lawyers and Accountants".
40. Author's interviews with Hayle, Vassell (16 November 2017) and Bernard (17 November 2017).
41. AR 2005–6, "Student Affairs", 23.
42. Author's interview with Vintoria Bernard, 27 November 2017, and Executive Director Rosemarie Heaven, 15 February 2018.
43. AR 2004–5, 20, and AR 2005–6, 22.
44. AR 2015–16, "President's Report", 9.
45. ICAC, Annual Report, 2013.
46. "AAT Jamaica to Be Formed", *ICAJ-N* (December 1988): 3.

47. Ibid., 3. "Accounting Technicians Analyse Figures, Often with a Bias Towards Specialist Work, such as Information Processing or Budgeting."
48. Ibid.
49. AR 1991, "Future of the Profession", 14.
50. AR 1993–94, "Association of Accounting Technicians (AAT)", 15–16.
51. AR 2001–2, "Student Affairs", 14.
52. CM, "Financial Report", February 2008.
53. Author's interview with Elizabeth Hartley, 21 February 2017.
54. Overseas Examinations Commission, "Report" (2008–9), 31.
55. AR 2012–13, "Student Affairs Committee", 21.
56. "Available Courses", https://studentvirtuallearn.accaglobal.com.
57. ICAJ, "Service Order 23 2 2016. Joint Foundations in Accountancy Suite of Qualifications"
58. Philmore Ogle, interview with the author, 2 March 2017.
59. Technicians Joint Examination Scheme Agreement between ICAJ and ACCA, 1 August 2003.
60. AR 1998–99, "President's Report" (Raphael Gordon), 11.
61. Operating Agreement, ICAJ/ACCA, 31 July 2008.
62. Patrick Bryan, *Administering Overseas Examinations in Jamaica: A History of the Overseas Examinations Commission, 1887–2007* (Kingston: Overseas Examinations Commission, 2014), 142.
63. AR 2009–10, 21.
64. Vintoria Bernard, interview with the author, 17 November 2017; Archibald Campbell, interview with the author, 21 November 2017.
65. Leighton McKnight, interview with the author, 26 January 2018.
66. AR 1999–2000, "ACCA Qualification Challenged", 8.
67. "Redesigning the Institute: ICAJ Puts the Right Foot Forward", *ICAJ-N* (July 2001): 4.
68. CM 27 June 2000, "CPA Perspective".
69. R 1999–2000, "ACCA Qualification Challenged", 8.
70. Ibid.
71. "ACCA Syllabus Forms UN Accounting Core", *ICAJ-N*, April 1999. The UN curriculum also included elements from the Certified General Accountants of Canada and educational guidelines from the International Federation of Accountants.
72. Carroll Thorburn to Jasper Burnett, 3 March 1980.
73. "CPA Perspective", 27 June 2000.
74. In 2014, the Canadian CMA and CGA were merged and renamed the CPA (Chartered Professional Accountants of Canada).
75. Sean Smith, "CGA: An Innovative Option to Achieve Our Career Goal", IACJ-N (July 2007): 9.

76. Ronald Mason, *Sunday Gleaner,* 28 September 2014.
77. See article *Daily Gleaner,* 25 June 2017, on the challenges of movement of personnel within the Caribbean.

Chapter 8

1. AR 2012–13, "The Building Project", 29.
2. "Notes to Financial Statements, 1999–2005", Statement 6, Note 15.
3. AR 1991, Table: "The Institute of Chartered Accountants of Jamaica", 10.
4. "Net Migration for Jamaica", FRED/St Louis Fed, Net Migration for Jamaica, https:// fred. St.Louis.org/Sertios/SMPOPP.NETMJ.
5. AR 2013–14, Note 24, "Notes to the Financial Statements", 31 March 2014, 59.
6. AR 2002–3, "Report of President Garth Kiddoe", 9.
7. AR 2015–16 Note 21, "Notes to the Financial Statements", 67. See also *ICAJ-N* (July 2011).
8. AR 2016–17, "Life Time Membership", 14.
9. Vintoria Bernard, interview with the author, 17 November 2017.
10. AR 2012–13, "Health Insurance Scheme", 11.
11. AR 2016–17, "Life Membership", 14.
12. C. Patricia Hayle, "Women as Today's Chartered Accountants 50 Years On" (unpublished paper, n.d.).
13. AR 2007–8, "National Outreach Sub-Committee", 9.
14. AR 2011–12, "Membership Outreach Sub-Committee", 19.
15. AR 2012–13, "Membership and Social Outreach Committee", 20.
16. Vintoria Bernard, interview with the author, 17 November 2017.
17. *Sunday Observer,* 10 December 2017, 2–3.
18. AR 2004–5, "ICAJ/UWI Cooperation Agreement", 11.
19. "MSc Reviewed", *ICAJ-N* (May 1997): 3.
20. AR 2014–15, "ICAJ/UWI Partnership", 14, and interview with Michael Williams, Mona School of Business and Management, 25 June 2021.
21. UWI, Departmental Reports, "Department of Management Studies", 2004–5, 341–42, and 2006–7, 364.
22. Ibid.
23. AR 2013–14, "Future of the Profession Committee", 17. See also, UWI, Mona, "Department of Management Studies, Departmental Report, 2006–07", 356. A central figure in boosting the internship programme has been Allison Peart.
24. Report of Student Affairs Committee to Council, 20 April 2006.
25. AR 2013–14, "Future of the Profession", 17.
26. ICAC, *Links Newsletter* (May–September 2017), 18.

Selected Bibliography

ICAJ Sources

ICAJ General Collection.

Jasper Burnett Working Papers.

Philmore Ogle Files.

Annual Reports of the ICAJ, 1977 to 2016.

ICAJ Newsletter, 1988–2016.

Charter magazine.

Minutes of Council, 1975–2016.

Press releases of the ICAJ.

ICAJ File: Speeches.

Aulous Madden (president, 1985–87). "Reflections: My Term in Office". Unpublished manuscript, n.d.

Public Accountancy Board Jamaica, *Rules and Regulations*. Kingston, 1968.

Interviews

Vintoria Bernard, 17 November 2017

Jasper Burnett, 23 February 2017

Archibald Campbell, 21 November 2017

Eric Crawford, 16 January 2018

Elizabeth Hartley, 21 February 2017

C. Patricia Hayle, 16 November 2017

Rosemarie Heaven, 15 February 2018

Garth Kiddoe, 19 January 2018

Alastair Macbeath, 19 January 2018

Aulous Madden, 16 January 2018

Linroy Marshall, 26 January 2018

Everton McDonald, 18 January 2018

Leighton McKnight, 26 January 2018

Philmore Ogle, 2 March 2017
Donald Reynolds, 12 January 2018
Bruce Scott, 29 November 2017
Prunella Vassell, 16 November 2017

Annisette, Marcia. "Imperialism and the Profession: The Education and Certification of Accountants in Trinidad and Tobago". *Accounting, Organizations and Society* 25 no. 7 (2000): 631–59.

Arnold, Patricia. "Disciplining Domestic Regulation: the World Trade Organization and the Market for Professional Services". *Accounting, Organizations and Society* 30 (2005): 299–330.

Bahl, Roy. "The Jamaican Tax Reform: Its Design and Performance". In *Tax Reform in Developing Countries,* edited by Wayne Thirsk, 167–231. Washington: World Bank, 1997.

Bakre, Owolabi. "Integration and Conflict of Identity: An Analysis of the Development of the Accountancy Profession in the Commonwealth Caribbean". A revised version of an earlier paper presented at the 7th Interdisciplinary Perspectives on Accounting Conference, Madrid, Spain, 13–16 July 2003.

Boxill, Ian. *Ideology and Caribbean Integration.* Kingston: Consortium Graduate School of Social Sciences, UWI, Mona, 1993.

Bryan, Patrick E. *Administering Overseas Examinations in Jamaica: A History of the Overseas Examinations Commission, 1887–2007.* Kingston: Overseas Examinations Commission, 2014.

———. *A History of the Caribbean Examinations Council, 1973–2013.* Bridgetown: Caribbean Examinations Council, 2015.

———. *The Jamaican People, 1880–2002. Race, Class and Social Control.* Kingston: University of the West Indies Press, 2000.

Burnett, Jasper, ed. *The Institute of Chartered Accountants of Jamaica: The First Twenty-Five Years, 1965–1990.* Kingston: The Institute of Chartered Accountants of Jamaica, 1990.

———. "Training of Accountants. A Discussion Paper between the Public Accountancy Board and the Council of the Institute of Chartered Accountants of Jamaica". 18 May 1982.

Cacho, C.P. "The Accountancy Profession in the Commonwealth Caribbean". Unpublished paper, 1968, Ogle Files, 1968.

Fortin, Henri, Ana Cristina Barros, and Kit Cutler. *Accounting for Growth in Latin America and the Caribbean. Improving Corporate Financial Reporting to Support Regional Economic Development.* Washington, DC: World Bank, 2010.

Goss, David. *Abolition and Plantation Management in Jamaica, 1807–1838.* Kingston: University of the West Indies Press, 2012.

Hall, Kenneth (ed). *Integrate or Perish! Perspectives of Leaders of the Integration Movement, 1963–1999.* Kingston: University of the West Indies/CARICOM Institutional Project, 2000.

Hartley, Elizabeth. "Report on the Future of the Students' Accountancy Training Consortium". Unpublished paper, n.d.

Hayle, C. Patricia. "Women as Today's Chartered Accountants 50 Years on". Unpublished paper, n.d.

Higman, B.W. *Plantation Jamaica, 1750–1850.* Kingston: University of the West Indies Press, 2005.

———. *Slave Population and Economy in Jamaica, 1807–1834.* Cambridge: Cambridge University Press, 1976.

Maria, T. Cristina. "The Impact of the Great Depression on American Accountancy Practice". *Annals of Faculty of Economics* 1, no. 2 (December 2012): 726–30.

McIntyre, Alister. *The Caribbean and the Wider World. Commentaries on My Life and Career.* Kingston: University of the West Indies Press, 2016.

Mendes, Margaret. "An Examination of Jamaica's Accountancy Training Problems and the Development of a Three Tiered Training Model as a Possible Solution". Unpublished manuscript, part 1 (September 1983) and part 2 (February 1984).

———. "Innovation in Professional Accountancy at the University of the West Indies Jamaica: 1968–88". MA (Education) thesis, 1990.

Mendes, Margaret, and Rachel McLean. *Regulatory Framework of Accounting in Jamaica.* Kingston: CFM, 1987. (3rd ed., 2001.)

Mills, Gladstone. *Grist for the Mills: Reflections on a Life.* Kingston: Ian Randle, 1994.

Mitchell, Keith, "Ninth Inter-Sessional Meeting St George's Grenada, 3 March, 1998" in *Integrate or Perish! Perspectives of Leaders of the Integration Movement, 1963 to 1999*, ed. Kenneth O. Hall, 559–62. Kingston: University of the West Indies/CARICOM Institutional Project, 2000.

Ogle, Philmore. "The Advent of the Institute". Unpublished paper, 2 July 2015.

Poullaos, Chris, and Suki Sian. *Accountancy and Empire: The British Legacy of Professional Organisation.* London: Routledge, 2010.

Preston, A.Z. "Address at the 21st Anniversary Banquet of the ICAJ held at the Pegasus on Saturday September 21, 1985". (ICAJ Archives).

Roberts, W. Adolphe. *These Many Years: An Autobiography*, ed. Peter Hulme. Kingston: University of the West Indies Press, 2015.

Sangster, Alfred. *The Making of a University: From CAST to UTech.* Kingston: Ian Randle, 2010.

Shackleton, Ken, and Stephen Walker. *Professional Reconstruction: The Coordination of the Accountancy Bodies, 1930–1957.* Edinburgh: Institute of Chartered Accountants of Scotland, 1998.

Wilson, Selby. "The Caribbean Accountants: Towards Integration". In *The Institute of Chartered Accountants: The First Twenty-Five Years*, ed. Jasper Burnett. Kingston: Institute of Chartered Accountants of Jamaica, 1990.

Index